W9-BIU-157

This book is available in quantity at special discounts for your group or organization. For further information, contact:

Triumph Books
601 South LaSalle Street
Suite 500
Chicago, Illinois 60605
(312) 939-3330
Fax (312) 663-3557

Project Editor: Luke Friend
Project Art Direction: Darren Jordan
Picture Research: Marc Glanville
Production: Lisa French
Design: Simon Mercer

Printed in the United States of America
ISBN 1-57243-540-2

NASCAR FANS GUIDE

THE ESSENTIAL INSIDER'S GUIDE TO WINSTON CUP RACING

Reid Spencer

Contents

ABOVE: Ricky Rudd in his No. 28 Ford and Jeremy Mayfield in his No. 19 Dodge battle for position during the Checker Auto Parts 500 at the Phoenix International Raceway.

introduction

ABOVE: Jimmie Johnson was one of the real stars of the 2002 Winston Cup Series, winning three times in his rookie season, and will be one to watch again in 2003.

NASCAR's Winston Cup Series enters the 2003 season with a unique set of circumstances and an abundance of unanswered questions.

Ironically, both series champion Tony Stewart and rookie of the year Ryan Newman will be driving different makes of cars from those that brought them their respective titles. Joe Gibbs Racing, which fielded Pontiacs for Stewart and 2000 Winston Cup champion Bobby Labonte in 2002, will switch allegiance Chevrolet in 2003—even though the Gibbs organization was an integral part of the development of the new Pontiac Grand Prix.

Newman and veteran teammate Rusty Wallace will drive Dodges next season, as owner Roger Penske opted to end his long-term association with Ford. The burning question in the Penske camp is this: Will the switch to the new model make it more difficult for Newman to repeat the sort of performance that saw him post one victory, six poles and 14 top fives in 2003, or will it propel him to even greater heights?

The Gibbs and Penske teams aren't the only major names changing manufacturers in 2003. Morgan-McClure Motorsports, long allied with Chevrolet, will switch to Pontiac, hoping that Gibbs' defection from the Grand Prix will bring more support from the factory to other Pontiac teams.

With the emergence of the high-profile Chevrolets of Dale Earnhardt, Inc., and the expansion of Richard Childress Racing to three cars in recent years, Morgan-McClure had fallen a few rungs in the Chevy pecking order.

Likewise, owner Cal Wells, who fields the No. 32 cars for driver Ricky Craven, will switch from Ford to Pontiac for the 2003 season. After all, Pontiacs have won two of the last three Winston Cup championships.

How much of a performance difference will all the switches from one manufacturer to another make? The conventional wisdom says probably not much. The new designs for 2003 embody a NASCAR's progression toward common templates for all the Winston Cup cars. Soon enough, race fans will have to read the label on the nose of a Winston Cup car to determine the manufacturer. Ironically, the sport that has long taken pride in brand identity is moving in a direction where the traditional brands will become indistinguishable one from another.

What will be clearly distinguishable during the 2003 season will be the drivers, particularly the youth movement that captivated fans of Winston Cup racing in 2002. Jimmie Johnson and Newman provided the most intense rookie-of-the-year battle in series history. Can they continue their phenomenal success as sophomore drivers? Can they match the performance of Kurt Busch, who enjoyed one of the most prolific second seasons in the history of the sport? Busch notched the first victory of his career at Bristol, then proceeded to win three of the last five events on the schedule to vault into third place in the final points standings.

Thirty-year-old Matt Kenseth and 31-year-old Jeff Gordon should again be part of the championship picture, provided Kenseth can overcome the inconsistencies that cost him a higher points finish in 2002, and provided Gordon can regain the focus that brought him his fourth Winston Cup title in 2001. The sooner Gordon can distance himself from the breakup of his seven-year marriage to wife Brooke, the better his performance on the track should be.

With the new wave of young drivers entering the sport, however, Gordon may be running short of time to equal or exceed the record of seven series championships shared by Richard Petty and the late Dale Earnhardt. Each year, Winston Cup racing grows increasingly competitive, and the number of drivers capable of winning races multiplies. The 2002 season was a perfect example. Johnson won three times as a rookie—matching Stewart's record for most wins as a first-year driver—and Newman won once.

Twenty-six-year-old Jamie McMurray, substituting for injured Sterling Marlin, won at Charlotte in his second career start, setting a modern-day record. And veteran Johnny Benson went to Victory Lane for the first time when he won the November race at Rockingham in his 226th career start.

Stock car racing aficionados will watch with interest to see whether McMurray will be able to duplicate his 2002 success in a Chip Ganassi-owned car that doesn't belong to Sterling Marlin. The No. 40 Coors Light Dodge, you'll remember, led the points standings after all but four races before Marlin was sidelined with a cracked vertebra at Kansas City. How the affable driver from Tennessee performs in 2003 after his recuperation will be one of the major stories of the coming season.

Another veteran, mark Martin, likewise will figure prominently in the 2003 campaign. Martin finished second in points for the fourth time in his career, but he proved conclusively to his doubters that he was still able and willing to race at the highest competitive level. Martin finished a mere 28 points behind Stewart, and that margin included a 25-point penalty assesses against Martin for an unapproved spring the No. 6 Viagra Ford team used during the fall race at Rockingham. (Ironically, that was the second time in Martin's career a penalty had affect the Arkansas driver's championship run. In 1990 he lost 46 points for a carburetor spacer infraction at Richmond—and lost the series title to Earnhardt by 26 points.)

The question about Martin involves durability. Though he's a fanatic about physical fitness, racing has taken its toll on his body, and he has experienced back problems in the past. Martin turns 44 before the 2003 season begins. Does he have enough left in the tank to mount another challenge for the championship, or was 2002 his swan song?

The 2002 season was one replete with driver and crew chief changes. There will be lots of familiar faces in unfamiliar cars when the field takes the green flag for the season-opening Daytona 500 in February. Particularly

ABOVE: Bill Elliott won twice in 2002 but the season was one of relative disappointment for Evernham Motorsports. They will be expecting better things in 2003.

noteworthy will be Elliott Sadler's debut in Robert Yates Racing's No. 38 Ford. The soap opera at Yates—complete with ill-disguised friction between veteran driver Ricky Rudd and ambitious young crew chief Michael McSwain—dominated Winston Cup headlines throughout the summer.

Ultimately, Rudd and Yates agreed to part ways at the end of the season, with Rudd agreeing to take Sadler's place behind the wheel of the Wood Brothers' No. 21 Ford. Soon after the announcement of Rudd's departure, McSwain negotiated his release from Yates and went to work for Gibbs, where he'll serve as crew chief for Bobby Labonte in 2003.

Labonte, though series champion in 2000, didn't enjoy the sort of success his teammate experienced in 2002. The hiring of McSwain, who will replace longtime crew chief Jimmy Makar on Labonte's pit box (though Makar will remain as team manager) was designed to restore a sense of cohesiveness within the No. 18 Interstate Batteries team. The big question is whether or not the personalities of laid-back Labonte and intense McSwain will mesh in a way that can produce optimum performance.

And while Labonte and McSwain are defining their relationship, Yates will attempt to return the No. 88 team of Dale Jarrett to the status of contender. The 1999 series champion, Jarrett suffered through a mediocre year in 2002. Though impossible to quantify, the turmoil on the Rudd side of the Yates' shop may have had an adverse effect on the Jarrett half of the equation.

Yates isn't the only veteran team with questions to answer in 2003. Richard Childress, who fielded the No. 3 Goodwrench Chevrolets for six of Earnhardt's seven championships, suffered through a season of frustration. His three-car operation could point to Jeff Green's 17th as the organizations best points finish. Not even a major personnel shakeup in late spring—when Robby Gordon and Kevin Harvick "traded" crew chiefs and pit crews—made a significant difference. Disenchanted with his 2002 results, Childress left the season finale at Homestead-Miami promising additional major changes involving his teams. Childress is a man of his word, so stay tuned for drastic action this season if Gordon, Harvick and Green continue to struggle.

If the results of the Childress cars were mediocre, the effort at vaunted Petty Enterprises was equally undistinguished. John Andretti struggled for the entire season and finished outside the top 25 in points for the second straight year. Buckshot Jones started the season in the No. 44 car but was released before mid-season to be replaced by a parade of journeyman drivers.

If there was a bright spot for the Petty organization, it was Kyle Petty himself. The 42-year-old son of stock car racing's King—Richard Petty—competed in every race and posted his best points finish since 1997. Petty will start the 2003 in the No. 45 car, with Andretti in the No. 43 (though Andretti finished the final race at Homestead with his contract for next year still unsigned.) Unproven Christian Fittipaldi, a convert from open-wheeled racing, will drive a limited schedule in the No. 44.

But can Petty—or Childress, for that matter—return to the championship level that once was both customary and expected? Or are their glory days behind them? Perhaps the most intriguing question for 2003 involves the prospects of Dale Earnhardt Jr. The enormity of Junior's talent is undeniable. At question is his ability to channel that talent into performances consistent enough to establish him as a championship contender. Earnhardt and DEI teammate Michael Waltrip have dominated restrictor-plate racing at NASCAR's two largest tracks, Daytona and Talladega. Earnhardt, in fact, has won the last three Winston

ABOVE: Petty Enterprises continued to struggle during the 2002 season though Kyle Petty did post his best points finish since 1997, finishing 22nd.

ABOVE: The 2002 season was the year Tony Stewart finally realized his potential, winning his first Winston Cup Championship. A repeat performance in 2003 would not come as a surprise.

Cup races held at Talladega, dating to 2001. But his results have been erratic at NASCAR's other venues, from the short tracks to the intermediate superspeedways to the road courses. And don't forget, Earnhardt has faced his share of adversity. Favored to win the 2000 rookie-of-the-year crown, he lost a close race to his friend, Matt Kenseth. In 2001, the unthinkable happened when his father died in a crash on the final lap of the Daytona 500. A concussion hampered his efforts in 2002. But 2003 brings the promise of a more focused run at the title. Tony Eury Jr. takes over as Junior's crew chief as Tony Eury Sr. assumes the duties of team manager. You can expect Earnhardt to finish better than 11th in points this year.

It's harder to determine what to expect from car owner Ray Evernham. The flagship Dodge team hasn't produced the results the manufacturer had hoped for or expected when Evernham left Hendrick Motorsports to form his organization. Though Bill Elliott won back-to-back race at Pocono and Indianapolis, the veteran driver finished outside the top 10 in points. Evernham and his second driver, Jeremy Mayfield, suffered through a frustrating season with one significant highlight, a second-place finish at Las Vegas. Expect some major shakeups in the Evernham camp if his teams don't get off to a strong start in 2003.

One thing is certain. Winston Cup teams will have less opportunity to gather information this year. NASCAR has reduced the number of test sessions each team can conduct at Winston Cup tracks from seven to five. That limitation should prove most painful for single-car operations, but you can expect the number of tests at non-Winston Cup venues (i.e., Greenville-Pickens or Kentucky Speedway) to increase in 2003.

Most unpredictable of all is Stewart, who clearly has the talent to win a second straight championship—if he can maintain his concentration on the task at hand. Despite winning NASCAR's top prize in 2002, the season was a tumultuous one for the Rushville Rocket, who made headlines for his temper tantrums off the track almost as often as he did for his accomplishments on the asphalt. Stewart and crew chief Greg Zipadelli have a solid working relationship. In fact, Stewart gave "Zippy" full credit for holding the Home Depot team together during its most volatile moments. If Stewart can harness his intensely competitive nature, he can be a champion many times over.

teams and drivers

NASCAR's Winston Cup Series is ready to roll into 2003 with one of the most controversial champions in the history of stock car racing. A driver with an abundance of talent, 2002 champion Tony Stewart has also gained considerable notoriety for his volatile nature off the track. The 2003 season will be perhaps the most wide open and unpredictable to date, with any number of drivers capable of winning the title. What follows is an analysis of their prospects.

RIGHT: The pit crews line up for another hard day's work.

NAPA
BENFIELD
WILSON
BARKER
Motorcraft
QUALITY PARTS
UAW
DELPHI
KERR
GRAY
NAPA
AUTO PARTS
POLLARD
J. GAY
KNAUER
PUNCH
LOWES

bill davis racing

Driver Ward Burton's victory in the Daytona 500 was the obvious highpoint to an otherwise unspectacular season for Bill Davis Racing.

One of the most affable and straightforward owners in the Winston Cup garage, Bill Davis has been searching for the secret to consistent performance for a decade. In 1993 and 1994, he fielded cars for Bobby Labonte, who went on to win a series championship in 2000. After auditioning a parade of drivers in 1995, the year Labonte moved left for greener pastures at Joe Gibbs racing, Davis settled on Ward Burton late in the season, and Burton promptly gave Davis his first victory as an owner at Rockingham. But Burton's best points finish under the Davis banner is ninth, again pointing to the team's need to be consistently, not just occasionally, competitive.

With one race left in the season, Burton and new crew chief Frankie Stoddard were still testing the waters together. The contrast was comical—Stoddard's rapid-fire, staccato New Hampshire patois in counterpoint to Burton's slow Virginia drawl.

The addition of Kenny Wallace as Burton's teammate should be of great help in 2003, given the opportunity to share testing information. Wallace is a good-natured driver, who like Burton, must find a way to harness his talent into consistent performances. From the owner down, the chemistry in the Davis organization should be positive. It would help, too, if Davis could find a few more dollars to buy a touch more speed.

TEAM STATISTICS

TEAM OWNER: BILL DAVIS

WARD BURTON	
Driver Number:	**No. 22**
Crew Chief:	**Frank Stoddard**
Team Sponsor:	**Caterpillar**

KENNY WALLACE	
Driver Number:	**No. 23**
Crew Chief:	**Philippe Lopez**
Team Sponsor:	**Hills Brothers Coffee**

ABOVE: Bill Davis is regarded as one of NASCAR's most likable and hardworking owners. He was rewarded in 2002 with a trip to Victory Lane in the Winston Cup's premier race—the Daytona 500.

Ward Burton

22

DRIVER STATISTICS

Burton ended the 2002 season in 25th place in the points standings. He scored two victories, three top-fives, eight top-10s and 17 top-20s.

DRIVER BIO	
Birth date:	**October 25, 1961**
Birthplace:	**South Boston, VA**
Team:	**Bill Davis Racing**
Sponsor:	**Caterpillar**
Owner:	**Bill Davis**
Crew Chief:	**Frank Stoddard**
Car:	**Dodge Intrepid**

CAREER RECORD	
Rookie Year:	**1994**
Starts:	**286**
Wins:	**5**
Top 5s:	**24**
Top 10s:	**75**
Money:	**$17,832,694**
Highlights:	**Winner of Daytona 500 2002.**

Daytona apart, 2002 was a frustrating ride for Burton.

It's just Ward Burton's luck. The highlight of his 2002 season came in the first official race, the Daytona 500. Not that Burton would trade his victory in NASCAR's most prestigious event for any other. But after the win at Daytona, Burton's season degenerated into a rapid downward spiral. True enough, Burton was third in the Winston Cup points standings after finishing seventh in the fourth event at Atlanta. Then the bottom dropped out, and Burton's free-fall was meteoric.

By mid-season, he had fallen to 25th, and not even a victory at New Hampshire in July could do much to buoy the No. 22 Caterpillar team. Heading into the final race of the season at Homestead-Miami Speedway, Burton had finished 40th or worse in seven of 35 races, a remarkable case of bad fortune. Three of those finishes were dead last (43rd), including consecutive events at the Dover and Kansas City where he was first to retire from the race.

Crew chief Tommy Baldwin, who had turned wrenches for Burton since 1998, left in frustration in September, to be replaced by garrulous Frank Stoddard (who was relieved of his crew chief duties at Roush Racing). With Stoddard on board, Burton managed a fifth-place finish at Martinsville, but the 2002 season had long since taken on the pale cast of mediocrity. However, it wasn't a total loss—it marked the first year Burton had won more than one race in a season. But Burton and Davis must develop at least the resemblance of consistency, if they ever hope to contend for a championship.

ABOVE: Burton won twice in 2002 but there was very little else to cheer about.

TOP LEFT: The key to 2003 for Burton and his crew will be consistency.

Kenny Wallace

ABOVE: The No. 23 Dodge was consistent if nothing else during the 2002 season.

BELOW RIGHT: Wallace will be hoping that 2003 brings him his first Winston Cup victory.

Security should help Wallace to a brighter season in 2003.

One of the more likable drivers in the garage area, Kenny Wallace finally found a home in Winston Cup racing in the latter half of the 2002 season. There were those who thought Wallace might be a candidate for the No. 1 Pennzoil Chevrolet fielded by DEI. After all, it was Wallace who substituted for injured Steve Park for the last three months of the 2001 season and the first four races of 2002. But Park returned in March, finished out the year amid rumors he would be released at the end of May and earned a one-year contract extension. That left Wallace, who had performed acceptably in his relief role, looking for another job.

He got fill-in work from Richard Childress at Martinsville, when NASCAR parked driver Kevin Harvick for an altercation with Greg Biffle after a Craftsman Truck Series race there. The following week he drove the No. 198 Aaron's Chevrolet at Talladega, finishing 21st. The Pepsi 400 at Daytona found Wallace in the No. 98 Stacker 2 Chevy, and he drove the same car to a 29th-place finish a week later at Chicagoland. The Stacker 2 car had two more undistinguished outings at Indianapolis and Watkins Glen before Davis hired Wallace to drive the No. 23 Hills Brothers Coffee Dodge in the Southern 500 at Darlington.

Wallace finished 25th at the "Lady in Black," but the next 10 races with Davis brought five top-20 finishes, including a 13th at Rockingham and an 11th at Phoenix. Wallace has never won a Winston Cup race and he posted his career-best points finish (22nd) in 1999. Clearly, he is looking for better things with Davis in 2003.

DRIVER STATISTICS

Wallace has secured a ride with Bill Davis Racing for 2003 and will be looking to improve on his 2002 season where he posted just one top-10 finish.

DRIVER BIO	
Birth date:	**August 23, 1963**
Birthplace:	**St. Louis, MO**
Team:	**Bill Davis Racing**
Sponsor:	**Hills Brothers Coffee**
Owner:	**Bill Davis**
Crew Chief:	**Bold**
Car:	**Dodge Intrepid**

CAREER RECORD	
Rookie Year:	**1993**
Starts:	**243**
Wins:	**0**
Top 5s:	**6**
Top 10s:	**26**
Money:	**$9,174,027**
Highlights:	**Career best points finish of 22nd in 1999.**

Chip Ganassi Racing

TEAM STATISTICS

TEAM OWNERS: CHIP GANASSI/FELIX SABATES

STERLING MARLIN	
Driver Number:	**No. 40**
Crew Chief:	**Lee McCall**
Team Sponsor:	**Coors Light**

Fate ends dream run for Ganassi/Marlin partnership.

Despite a strong performance from his top driver, and an unexpected victory from an unexpected source, the 2002 season was a pain in the neck for team owner Chip Ganassi. More accurately, perhaps, it was a pain in the neck for Sterling Marlin, who saw his bid for a Winston Cup championship disappear when he cracked a veterbra below the base of his skull during a brutal crash at Kansas City.

Enter Jamie McMurray, who will drive for Ganassi full-time in 2003. In his second Winston Cup start, while substituting for Marlin, McMurray won at Charlotte and quickly established himself as the leading contender for the rookie-of-the-year title in 2003. McMurray won't be driving the Coors Light Dodge, however. He'll be behind the wheel of Ganassi's Chevron Dodge, carrying either the No. 28 or No. 42.

Ganassi will also field the No. 41 Dodge in 2003, but as of the final week of the 2002 season, he had yet to name a driver. With two weeks left in the season, Ganassi informed Jimmy Spencer that the Homestead race would be Spencer's last in the No. 41. Spencer had one year and one option year left on his contract with Ganassi Racing, and the two principals were to work out the details of their separation after the final race. Leading contenders for the seat were said to include Bobby Hamilton, who parted with Andy Petree Racing after the 2002 season, and open-wheeled racing star Jimmy Vasser.

ABOVE: Consistently strong pit-work by the Ganassi crew helped Marlin lead the Winston Cup standings for 25 weeks with a string of competitive runs.

Sterling Marlin 40

Marlin's best-ever season ends early after a job well done.

The story of Sterling Marlin's 2002 season is one of triumph—and of heartbreak. After a third-place finish in points in 2001 in his first full year driving for Chip Ganassi, a year in which he established himself as the leading Dodge driver in the Winston Cup Series, Marlin was one of the favorites to contend for the championship in 2002. The handicappers weren't wrong. In short order, Marlin seized the lead in the points standings, despite a *faux pas* in the season-opening Daytona 500, when he climbed from his car under a red-flag condition and attempted to pull his right front fender away from the tire it was rubbing.

That violation of NASCAR rules may have cost Marlin victory, but it wasn't long before he won his first race of the season. After a runner-up finish at Rockingham to follow his eighth at Daytona, Marlin took the checkered flag at Las Vegas and assumed the Winston Cup Series lead.

He held the top spot in the standings for 25 weeks, but a hard crash at Richmond in September spelled the beginning of the end for the 45-year-old Tennessee driver. He wasn't in top form at New Hampshire and Dover, and he fell to fourth in points after the latter race.

The following week brought the *coup de grace*. After a violent wreck at Kansas Speedway, doctors discovered that Marlin's C-2 veterbra, at the base of the skull, was broken, and his championship run was over.

One of the most gracious drivers in the Winston Cup garage, Marlin accepted his misfortune philosophically and vowed to renew his challenge in 2003. With Ganassi behind him, he just might occupy the seat at the champions' table he seemed destined to hold in 2002.

ABOVE: The No. 40 Coors Light car gave veteran Marlin his best ever run at the Winston Cup.

BELOW LEFT: Marlin was left to ponder what might have been, and what could be next year.

DRIVER STATISTICS

Marlin rolled over his fine 2001 form to this season. With two wins, eight top-fives and 14 top-10s from 29 starts he looked set for a championship run before his Kansas accident.

DRIVER BIO	
Birth date:	**June 30, 1957**
Birthplace:	**Franklin, TN**
Team:	**Chip Ganassi Racing**
Sponsor:	**Coors Light**
Owner:	**Chip Ganassi/Felix Sabates**
Crew Chief:	**Lee McCall**
Car:	**Dodge Intrepid**

CAREER RECORD	
Rookie Year:	**1983**
Starts:	**568**
Wins:	**10**
Top 5s:	**79**
Top 10s:	**192**
Money:	**$23,528,534**
Highlights:	**Winner of 1994-95 Daytona 500. Rookie of the Year 1983.**

dale earnhardt inc.

ABOVE: The No. 8 Chevy has shown impressive speed on the super-fast restrictor plate tracks, but if the team is to win consistently in 2003 it must up its all-round game.

TEAM STATISTICS

TEAM OWNER: TERESA EARNHARDT

STEVE PARK	
Driver Number:	**No. 1**
Crew Chief:	**Tony Gibson**
Team Sponsor:	**Pennzoil**
DALE EARNHARDT JR.	
Driver Number:	**No. 8**
Crew Chief:	**Tony Eury Sr.**
Team Sponsor:	**Budweiser**
MICHAEL WALTRIP	
Driver Number:	**No. 15**
Crew Chief:	**Richard 'Slugger' Labbe**
Team Sponsor:	**NAPA Auto Parts**

High-speed highlights cannot cover general shortcomings.

The folks at DEI have made their point. They can dominate the restrictor-plate races on NASCAR's largest tracks but can they win consistently enough on the Winston Cup's shorter venues to challenge for the championship?

The focus at DEI clearly is on Dale Earnhardt Jr. and his Budweiser Chevy. After all, it's Earnhardt's name that is on the door. Despite two victories at Talladega, however, Earnhardt suffered through an inconsistent season and never was a serious challenger for the championship. With an experienced crew led by Tony Eury Sr., Junior ought to do better.

Michael Waltrip has garnered two restrictor-plate victories in the past two seasons, both at Daytona. But Waltrip seems to drive his best when his job's on the line. Crew chief Slugger Labbe has an additional job that might be just as important as anything he does in the pits—keeping the whimsical Waltrip motivated. The guy can drive when he wants to.

Despite persistent rumors that Steve Park would be fired before the end of the 2002 season, team owner Teresa Earnhardt gave the 35-year-old driver a one-year contract extension in August. It was a season of adversity for Park, who missed the first four races during his recovery from a head injury suffered at Darlington in September of 2001. Crew chief Paul Andrews departed in September to call the shots for Jeff Burton at Roush Racing, ultimately to be replaced by Tony Gibson.

Dale Earnhardt Jr. 8

DRIVER STATISTICS

Junior won twice in 2002—both at Talladega—and recorded 11 top-fives and 16 top-10s. Despite earning over four millions dollars for the season, he finished 11th in points.

DRIVER BIO	
Birth date:	**October 10, 1974**
Birthplace:	**Concord, NC**
Team:	**Dale Earnhardt**
Sponsor:	**Budweiser**
Owner:	**Teresa Earnhardt**
Crew Chief:	**Tony Eury Sr.**
Car:	**Chevrolet Monte Carlo**

CAREER RECORD	
Rookie Year:	**2000**
Starts:	**111**
Wins:	**7**
Top 5s:	**23**
Top 10s:	**37**
Money:	**$13,096,538**
Highlights:	**Busch Series champion 1998–99. Recorded two wins in rookie season.**

"Little E" lives up to his father's name, but no title challenge yet.

In his third full year of Winston Cup racing, Dale Earnhardt Jr. already has established himself as THE dominant player on the restrictor-plate superspeedways his late father had mastered. In October 2002, Earnhardt Jr. posted his second victory of the season at Talladega Superspeedway, giving him three straight wins at NASCAR's largest track and four victories in the six restrictor-plate races dating to his emotional win in the Pepsi 400 in July of 2001.

But aside from the "plate" races, 2002 was an uneven year for "Little E," who saw his season fall apart during a brutal stretch of seven races immediately preceding the Pepsi 400. Back-to-back 36th-place finishes at California and Richmond started a free-fall that would drop him to 16th after a 30th-place result at Sonoma's road course on June 23. A sixth in the Pepsi 400, a third at Bristol, a fourth at Richmond, another sixth at Kansas City, the second win at Talladega and a fourth at Martinsville brightened the picture considerably, but by then a strong points finish was beyond reach.

Earnhardt's improvement during the latter half of the season, however, should inspire confidence that a championship is a distinct possibility. To bolster the team for a title run in 2003, DEI plans to move David Charpentier to the No. 8 Budweiser team as chief engineer.

The real question mark is whether Earnhardt and company can find a consistent performance level on short and intermediate tracks that at least will approach their prowess on the restrictor-plate circuits.

ABOVE: A mid-season bad patch dropped the No. 8 Chevy out of championship contention.
TOP: Earnhardt Jr. took both of his 2002 victories at the daunting Talladega Speedway.

Steve Park

Park promise shows through despite a patchy year.

Near the end of a difficult 2002 season, Steve Park appeared to be making progress—an encouraging sign for a driver who twice has returned from serious injuries suffered on the track.

Not sufficiently recovered from post-concussion syndrome (the result of a hard crash during a Busch Series race at Darlington on Sept. 1, 2001), Park missed the first four races of the 2002 season before returning to action in the spring, ironically enough, at Darlington. Park qualified fourth but an accident relegated him to a 39th place finish. The next few months were a struggle, but the 35-year-old driver from East Northport, N.Y., came home seventh in the Brickyard 400 at Indianapolis. Five events later, at Richmond, he finished 11th. At the October race at Talladega, he drove to the front of the pack and a sixth-place result.

Park is all too familiar with the rigors of rehabilitation. In his 1998 rookie season, he missed 15 races because of injuries suffered in a crash. It wasn't until 2000 that the driver handpicked by the late Dale Earnhardt won his first Winston Cup race, on the road course at Watkins Glen. The week after Earnhardt died at the 2001 Daytona 500, Park gave DEI its second straight win with his victory at Rockingham.

The No. 1 Pennzoil team suffered another setback in September of 2002 when veteran crew chief Paul Andrews resigned.

How Park fares in 2003 will depend on his ability to put the effects of a major accident behind him—for the second time in his career.

ABOVE: After retaking his seat from Mike Wallace, Park qualified fourth for his return at Darlington.

BELOW LEFT: Park was considered fortunate to retain his drive for 2003.

DRIVER STATISTICS

After missing the first four races of the 2002 season, Park recorded three top-fives and three top-10s, helping him to a 33rd spot in the points standings.

DRIVER BIO	
Birth date:	**August 23, 1967**
Birthplace:	**East Northport, NY**
Team:	**Dale Earnhardt Inc.**
Sponsor:	**Pennzoil**
Owner:	**Teresa Earnhardt**
Crew Chief:	**Tony Gibson**
Car:	**Chevrolet Monte Carlo**

CAREER RECORD	
Rookie Year:	**1998**
Starts:	**146**
Wins:	**2**
Top 5s:	**11**
Top 10s:	**32**
Money:	**$9,790,144**
Highlights:	**First Winston Cup win in 2000. Busch Series Rookie of the Year 1997.**

Michael Waltrip

Waltrip's mixed motivation leads to up-and-down-season.

The best thing Dale Earnhardt Incorporated can do for Michael Waltrip is to find a way to keep him uncomfortable—and motivated.

After a fifth-place finish in the seasoning-opening Daytona 500 in 2002, Waltrip fell off the map. Two engine failures in the first four events didn't help, and when the Winston Cup Series left Texas Motor Speedway after the April 7 race there, Waltrip was a dismal 27th in points.

That's when the rumors began to surface—that DEI might not renew Waltrip's contract beyond the 2002 season. Perhaps it's just coincidence, but with his job reportedly on the line, Waltrip found a higher gear. He finished 13th at Martinsville and roared to a second-place finish behind Dale Earnhardt Jr. a week later at Talladega. The next six races brought four top-10 finishes, and Waltrip moved up the charts faster than a new Garth Brooks single. Waltrip's string of success culminated in the second victory of his career in a Winston Cup points race in the July 6 Pepsi 400 at Daytona. It wasn't long before DEI opted to renew the 39-year-old driver's contract for 2003.

Again, it may just be coincidence, but with Waltrip's comfort level reestablished, his performance began to slip. Ultimately, he found his niche at or around 15th in the points for the latter half of the season.

For 2003, Waltrip needs a goal—to finish as strongly as he starts. Perhaps DEI should give him the incentive he needs by hiring Waltrip on a week-to-week basis. He might just win a championship.

ABOVE: Waltrip is unbeatable when the mood takes him, but he wasn't in the zone often enough.

BELOW: Speculation on his DEI future spurred Waltrip to great heights on occasion.

DRIVER STATISTICS

Waltrip recorded the second win of his career in 2002 on his way to a 14th place finish in the points standings. He also posted four top-fives and 10 top-10s.

DRIVER BIO

Birth date:	**April 30, 1963**
Birthplace:	**Owensboro, KY**
Team:	**Dale Earnhardt Inc.**
Sponsor:	**NAPA Auto Parts**
Owner:	**Teresa Earnhardt**
Crew Chief:	**Richard "Slugger" Labbe**
Car:	**Chevrolet Monte Carlo**

CAREER RECORD

Rookie Year:	**1984**
Starts:	**534**
Wins:	**2**
Top 5s:	**25**
Top 10s:	**95**
Money:	**$17,614,956**
Highlights:	**Winner of Daytona 500 2001.**

Evernham Motorsports

The 2002 season produced mixed results for Evernham. They had their victories but lacked the consistency they had hoped for.

When Ray Evernham left Hendrick Motorsports to spearhead Dodge's return to Winston Cup racing, most followers of the sport expected him to field the top team for that car make. Instead, owner Chip Ganassi has headed the top-performing Dodge outfit, with Sterling Marlin leading the points standings for most of the 2002 season (before a cracked vertebra sidelined the Tennessee driver).

Admittedly, Evernham and driver Bill Elliott have turned in some outstanding performances. The 45-year-old driver, whose career was rejuvenated when he signed with Evernham for the 2001 season, won back-to-back races at Pocono and Indianapolis, but the team struggled with consistency. Elliott stood as high as sixth in points after the victory at the Brickyard, but the last four months of the season were unkind to "Awesome Bill," who eventually dropped out of the top 10.

In addition, Evernham and Jeremy Mayfield failed to achieve the results they expected. Mayfield dropped as far as 28th in points after an engine failure at the Brickyard, and for the season, he finished 35th or worse more often than he finished in the top 10. Dave Skog is listed as the crew chief of the No. 19 Dodge—after the departure of Sammy Johns to head Evernham's research and development effort—but in reality, the Mayfield crew pitted the car by committee. That should change in 2003 with the naming of a new pit boss.

TEAM STATISTICS

TEAM OWNER: RAY EVERNHAM

BILL ELLIOTT	
Driver Number:	**No. 9**
Crew Chief:	**Mike Ford**
Team Sponsor:	**Dodge Dealers**

JEREMY MAYFIELD	
Driver Number:	**No. 19**
Crew Chief:	**Dave Skog**
Team Sponsor:	**Dodge Dealers**

ABOVE: Bill Elliott's pit crew—headed by crew chief Mike Ford—has teamed up well with their driver, winning twice in 2002 in the No. 9 Dodge.

Bill Elliott

Elliott still in the swing of things after a strong season.

It had been years since "Awesome Bill" Elliott had been awesome. Winless since 1994 when he joined Ray Evernham's flagship Dodge operation for the 2001 season, the 47-year-old Dawsonville, Ga., driver was a question mark. Was he a driver who would merely run out the string on a waning career, or would Elliott regain the form that propelled him to a Winston Cup championship in 1988?

That Evernham had hired him in the first place was a vote of confidence for Elliott, who at the peak of his career in 1985 had won 11 races and 11 poles—not to mention the first "Winston Million" bonus. From 1995 through 2002, Elliott had struggled as an owner/driver without a single visit to Victory Lane during those six seasons.

Elliott finished the 2001 season 15th in points and as he and Evernham became more comfortable with their working relationship, he continued to improve his results in 2002. He won poles at Atlanta and Texas and finished fourth and second, respectively at California and Dover. Elliott returned to Victory Lane at Pocono in late July, and a week later, he added his name to the list of winners of the Brickyard 400 at Indianapolis. He remained solidly in the top 10 in points until a 42nd-place finish at Martinsville dropped him to 11th late in the season.

With Mike Ford on his pit box as an effective, low-key crew chief, and with Evernham's wisdom and resources behind him, Elliott could make a concerted run at the Winston Cup title in 2003.

ABOVE: Elliott capped off some strong first-half drives with consecutive wins at Pocono and Indy.

BELOW: Although his best days are behind him, Elliott can still race with the best of them.

DRIVER STATISTICS

Elliott recorded back-to-back wins in 2002 to go alongside six top-fives, 13 top-10s and 23 top-20s. He finished the season 13th in the points standings.

DRIVER BIO	
Birth date:	**October 8, 1955**
Birthplace:	**Dawsonville, GA**
Team:	**Evernham Sports**
Sponsor:	**Dodge Dealers**
Owner:	**Ray Evernham**
Crew Chief:	**Mike Ford**
Car:	**Dodge Intrepid**

CAREER RECORD	
Rookie Year:	**1976**
Starts:	**695**
Wins:	**43**
Top 5s:	**166**
Top 10s:	**307**
Money:	**$30,976,107**
Highlights:	**Winston Cup champion 1988. First winner of the 'Winston Million.'**

Jeremy Mayfield

19

High hopes turn sour for Evernham/Mayfield link-up.

Doubtless Jeremy Mayfield had hoped for a better inaugural season when he signed on with Ray Evernham for the 2002 campaign. Mayfield came to Evernham's Dodge operation with three Winston Cup victories to his credit but hadn't won a race since his dramatic last-lap "bump" against the late Dale Earnhardt at Pocono in 2000.

But Mayfield had shown enormous promise with Penske, and the 33-year-old driver from Owensboro, Ky., expected no small degree of success with Evernham in 2002. But reality was a far cry from those expectations. A woeful start to the season saw Mayfield finish 39th in the Daytona 500 and 29th a week later at Rockingham. When he finished second to Sterling Marlin at Las Vegas in the season's third race, however, Mayfield leap-frogged from 36th to 18th in the Winston Cup points standings. The good fortune didn't last. With the exception of a fifth at Richmond, Mayfield didn't crack the top 10 again until September's event at Dover.

Mayfield started the season with Sammy Johns as crew chief, but Johns left the position to head Evernham's research-and-development effort. For much of the season, Mayfield's team has been working on the car by committee, though Dave Skog held the title of crew chief.

Despite an overall lackluster performance, Mayfield showed progress as the 2002 season came to an end. Over the last three months, he improved his average finish by roughly four positions. Both Mayfield and Evernham believe that a year of experience together will make the team a much more formidable contender in 2003.

ABOVE: The No. 19 Dodge was rarely seen at the sharp end in 2002.

BELOW LEFT: Mayfield will be looking for a return to Victory Lane in 2003.

DRIVER STATISTICS

Mayfield struggled through a frustrating 2002 Winston Cup season. He failed to win and could only post two top-fives and four top-10s on his way to a 26th place in the points standings.

DRIVER BIO	
Birth date:	**May 27, 1969**
Birthplace:	**Mooresville, NC**
Team:	**Evernham Motorsports**
Sponsor:	**Dodge Dealers**
Owner:	**Ray Evernham**
Crew Chief:	**Dave Skog**
Car:	**Dodge Intrepid**

CAREER RECORD	
Rookie Year:	**1994**
Starts:	**273**
Wins:	**3**
Top 5s:	**35**
Top 10s:	**61**
Money:	**$14,223,793**
Highlights:	**Two wins in 2000. Seventh in Winston Cup points 1998.**

Hendrick Motorsports

Armed with Gordon and Johnson, Hendrick will always be a threat.

The facts don't lie. Hendrick Motorsports has been the most successful team in Winston Cup racing during the past decade. Indeed, the Hendrick cars have won five of the last eight series championships. Admittedly, Jeff Gordon is responsible for four of those, and there's no doubt that the departure of Gordon's former crew chief, Ray Evernham, made for a difficult transition within the stock car racing powerhouse, but Hendrick still possesses the know-how and the resources to produce one or more contenders each season.

The 2002 season was a perfect example. Rookie Jimmie Johnson, driver a car owned by Gordon in partnership with Hendrick, won three races (tying Tony Stewart's record for a first-year driver) and actually held the points lead after the Kansas City race on Sept. 29. Johnson and crew chief Chad Knaus proved a brilliant combination. Driver Joe Nemechek and crew chief Peter Sospenzo are under contract with Hendrick for 2003—and are excited to be there. The biggest challenge for the organization will be to help two-time champion Terry Labonte rediscover the speed that seems to have deserted him.

Hendrick Motorsports will also provide technical assistance to Haas CNC Motorsports and driver Jack Sprague next season. Sprague, who drove for Hendrick in the Craftsman Truck Series and Busch Series, will run for the Winston Cup rookie-of-the-year title in 2003.

ABOVE: Jeff Gordon couldn't bring home another Winston Cup championship for Hendrick Motorsports in 2002 but he will surely challenge again in 2003.

TEAM STATISTICS

TEAM OWNER: RICK HENDRICK

JEFF GORDON	
Driver Number:	**No. 24**
Crew Chief:	**Robbie Loomis**
Team Sponsor:	**DuPont**

JIMMIE JOHNSON	
Driver Number:	**No. 48**
Crew Chief:	**Chad Knaus**
Team Sponsor:	**Lowe's**

TERRY LABONTE	
Driver Number:	**No. 5**
Crew Chief:	**Jim Long**
Team Sponsor:	**Kellogg's**

JOE NEMECHEK	
Driver Number:	**No. 25**
Crew Chief:	**Peter Sospenzo**
Team Sponsor:	**UAW/Delphi**

Jeff Gordon

24

DRIVER STATISTICS

For a four-time champion, Gordon's 2002 season was a little frustrating—but the numbers were still impressive, including three wins, 13 top-fives and 20 top-10s.

DRIVER BIO	
Birth date:	**August 4, 1971**
Birthplace:	**Vallejo, CA**
Team:	**Hendrick Motorsports**
Sponsor:	**Dupont**
Owner:	**Rick Hendrick**
Crew Chief:	**Robbie Loomis**
Car:	**Chevrolet Monte Carlo**

CAREER RECORD	
Rookie Year:	**1993**
Starts:	**329**
Wins:	**61**
Top 5s:	**160**
Top 10s:	**210**
Money:	**$50,729,750**
Highlights:	**Winston Cup champion 2001, 1998, 1997, 1995.**

ABOVE: Gordon continued to win in 2002 but he lacked his usual consistency.

TOP RIGHT: Look for Gordon to bounce back in 2003 with another run at the championship.

Off-track distractions deny Gordon back-to-back titles.

Defending Winston Cup champion Jeff Gordon couldn't quite get the job done when it counted in 2002. A botched pit stop here, a blown motor there, and Gordon had missed a golden opportunity to win back-to-back championships for the second time in his career.

Perhaps the breakup of his seven-year marriage to wife Brooke was too much of a distraction. Shepherding rookie Jimmie Johnson's championship bid (on a team co-owned by Gordon and Rick Hendrick) also required his attention.

It was an unusual season in which the title was there for the taking, but Gordon—uncharacteristically—was unable to respond to the opportunity. That he was even a contender until very late in the season was surprising, given that the 31-year-old California native was suffering through the longest drought of his career. Gordon's winless streak reached 36 races before he broke it with a victory at Bristol on Aug. 24. He followed that with his fifth Southern 500 victory at Darlington a week later and climbed to second in points behind Sterling Marlin.

But Gordon's advance toward the top of the standings was short-lived with a blown motor at Charlotte on Oct. 13 finally eliminating him from the championship picture.

Bear in mind, though, that Gordon rarely has two less-than-stellar seasons in a row. He has the full weight of Hendrick's resources behind him and, if 2003 presents the opportunity for a fifth Winston Cup title, chances are that Gordon will seize it.

jimmie johnson

Johnson compiles a rookie season for the ages in 2002.

Who could have guessed that rookie Jimmie Johnson would have outshone his car owner and mentor, defending Winston Cup champion Jeff Gordon, in 2002? Johnson made the most of his opportunity to drive for Gordon and co-owner Rick Hendrick. In one of the most exciting rookie-of-the-year battles in Winston Cup history, Johnson won three races—one at California and two at Dover—to tie Tony Stewart's record number of victories in a rookie campaign.

What's more, Johnson was a contender for the series championship, an almost unheard-of feat for a first-year driver, until a mishap on a pace lap at Talladega dropped him from the points lead.

At the start of the season, Johnson gave an immediate indication that this would be no ordinary rookie season. He won the pole for the Daytona 500 and finished 15th. He followed that performance with a run of five straight top-10s. Johnson won at California in the 10th race of the season and returned to Victory Lane at Dover three races later. When an early crash at Kansas City knocked Sterling Marlin out of the race, Johnson assumed the points lead. Though he ended his rookie season fifth in the Winston Cup standings, seven points ahead of fellow first-year competitor Ryan Newman, it was Newman who won the Rookie-of-the-Year title thanks to a more consistent performance.

Nevertheless, Johnson clearly established himself as a championship contender, and with gifted crew chief Chad Knaus calling the shots in the pits, Johnson should be a factor in the title race for years to come.

ABOVE: Johnson more than repaid the faith put in him by owners Jeff Gordon and Rick Hendrick.

BELOW LEFT: After an awesome 2002, Johnson will be hoping the sequel is just as successful.

DRIVER STATISTICS

Johnson won three times in his rookie season and posted six top-fives and 21 top-10s on his way to a fifth place points standing and $2,697,702.

DRIVER BIO	
Birth date:	**September 17, 1975**
Birthplace:	**El Cajon, CA**
Team:	**Hendrick Motorsports**
Sponsor:	**Lowe's**
Owner:	**Rick Hendrick/Jeff Gordon**
Crew Chief:	**Chad Knaus**
Car:	**Chevrolet Monte Carlo**

CAREER RECORD	
Rookie Year:	**2002**
Starts:	**39**
Wins:	**3**
Top 5s:	**6**
Top 10s:	**21**
Money:	**$2,970,020**
Highlights:	**Three wins in 2002. Rookie of the Year runner-up 2002.**

Joe Nemechek

25

DRIVER STATISTICS

Nemechek made 33 starts in 2002. He didn't record a victory but did register three top-fives and three top-10s, enough to secure a ride for Hendrick Motorsports in 2003.

DRIVER BIO	
Birth date:	**September 26, 1963**
Birthplace:	**Naples, FL**
Team:	**Hendrick Motorsports**
Sponsor:	**UAW-Delphi**
Owner:	**Rick Hendrick**
Crew Chief:	**Peter Sospenzo**
Car:	**Chevrolet Monte Carlo**

CAREER RECORD	
Rookie Year:	**1994**
Starts:	**286**
Wins:	**2**
Top 5s:	**11**
Top 10s:	**35**
Money:	**$12,280,036**
Highlights:	**Busch Series champion 1992. First Winston Cup victory in 1999.**

ABOVE: "Front Row Joe" will be looking to turn his qualifying success into wins in 2003.

BELOW LEFT: The No. 25 UAW-Delphi car provides Nemechek with a opportunity to impress.

Hard work lands Nemechek a premier ride for 2003.

Joe Nemechek landed his latest Winston Cup ride the old-fashioned way—he earned it. Nemechek will start the 2003 Winston Cup season in the same car in which he ended the 2002 campaign—the No. 25 UAW/Delphi Chevrolet owned by Rick Hendrick. At the start of the 2002 season, however, driving for Hendrick was the farthest thing from Nemechek's mind. He was more interested to see whether or not backing could be found to sustain his position with Travis Carter.

Hired by Carter as a teammate for Todd Bodine, Nemechek soon learned that the team would run out of sponsorship money two races into the 2002 season because of the bankruptcy of Carter's primary sponsor, Kmart. Carter nevertheless kept Nemechek on the track for the first six races of the season while he looked for a new sponsor. Nemechek, whose 17th-place finish in the spring race at Darlington was his best for Carter in 2002, missed races at Texas, Martinsville and Talladega but returned for his swan song with Carter in the 10th event of the season at California. By then, the well was dry.

The 39-year-old Nemechek, known as "Front Row Joe" for his prowess in qualifying, was impressive as a substitute for injured Johnny Benson at Richmond, where Nemechek qualified 16th and finished 12th. That performance happened to coincide roughly with the release of Jerry Nadeau from Hendrick's No. 25 Chevrolet, and Nemechek inherited the ride. He spent the rest of the season auditioning for full-time employment. A fourth-place finish at Kansas City and a second at Atlanta

solidified his chances. Another factor that no doubt influenced Hendrick in the hiring of Nemechek was the performance of the team after veteran crew chief Peter Sospenzo came aboard on Sept. 10. Both Nemechek and Sospenzo got the word that they had been retained for the 2003 season during the week before the season's final race.

terry Labonte

Mr. Consistency winless for third year in a row.

Terry Labonte has always been a model of consistency. Of late, however, Labonte's performances have declined from consistently excellent to consistently mediocre. It's probably fair to say that Labonte hasn't been the same since the grinding crash that took the 46-year-old Texas driver out of the 2000 Pepsi 400 at Daytona. Injuries he suffered in that wreck caused Labonte to miss subsequent races thereby ending his record streak of 655 consecutive Winston Cup starts.

The 2002 season showed signs of improvement, but they were hardly dramatic. Labonte did manage to lead 11 laps at Martinsville, where he finished sixth in the spring race, and he found some of his old road course magic at Sonoma, where he finished third. Labonte was 16th in points after the Brickyard 400, but a disastrous late-season slump, during which he finished 30th or worse in eight of nine races (ending with Talladega), dropped him to 23rd in the points standings.

Never a prolific winner on the Winston Cup circuit, Labonte earned his keep by taking care of his equipment and accumulating top-five results. In each of his two championship seasons, Labonte won only two races, but in 1984 he collected 17 top-fives and, en route to the 1996 title, he finished second seven times and posted 21 top-fives.

Winston Cup's Iron Man has a capable crew chief in Jim Long. He also has the resources of Hendrick Motorsports behind him. If Labonte can't find some speed during the 2003 season, it may be time for him to hang up the driving shoes.

ABOVE: Too often Labonte couldn't hit the No. 5 Chevy's sweet spot.

BELOW RIGHT: Former champ Labonte will be out to end his winless streak in 2003.

DRIVER STATISTICS

The 2002 season saw Labonte winless and he posted only one top-five finish. He finished the year 24th in the points standings, winning $3,064,935.

DRIVER BIO	
Birth date:	**November 16, 1956**
Birthplace:	**Corpus Christi, TX**
Team:	**Hendrick Motorsports**
Sponsor:	**Kellog's**
Owner:	**Rick Hendrick**
Crew Chief:	**Jim Long**
Car:	**Chevrolet Monte Carlo**

CAREER RECORD	
Rookie Year:	**1979**
Starts:	**745**
Wins:	**21**
Top 5s:	**177**
Top 10s:	**344**
Money:	**$29,680,682**
Highlights:	**Two-time Winston Cup champion (1984, 1996).**

Jasper Racing

ABOVE: Jasper Racing and driver Dave Blaney are proof that you can remain competitive in the Winston Cup Series without huge funding.

Despite lack of funds, Jasper and Blaney both achieved career highs in 2002.

In a move that proved productive for both parties, Dave Blaney joined Jasper Motorsports for the 2002 season, and drove the No. 77 Taurus to its best points finish ever. Blaney himself also achieved a personal best in his third full season of Winston Cup racing and cracked the top-20 in the standings for the first time.

The team received a blow late in the season, however, when crew chief Ryan Pemberton—one of the most imaginative pit bosses in the garage—announced he was leaving Jasper for MB2 Motorsports and driver Jerry Nadeau. Pemberton's departure fueled rumors that Blaney might defect to Chip Ganassi's organization to replace fired Jimmy Spencer in the No. 41 Dodge. But Blaney put those rumors to rest by renewing his contract with Jasper owner Doug Bawel before the final race of 2002 at Homestead-Miami.

Jasper Motorsports is a single-car team without massive funding. Consequently, the choice of a crew chief to replace Pemberton will be crucial to the team's success. But as Blaney, a former sprint car champion, gains experience and continues to adapt from open wheels to stock cars, the outlook for Jasper is promising. Though a pair of ninth-place finishes were Blaney's best entering the final race of 2002, he exhibited a level of consistency that eluded many other drivers in the series—despite finishing no better than ninth, Blaney posted an average result of 20.617.

TEAM STATISTICS

TEAM OWNER: DOUG BAWEL

DAVE BLANEY	
Driver Number:	**No. 77**
Crew Chief:	**Ryan Pemberton**
Team Sponsor:	**Jasper Engines and Transmissions**

dave blaney

DRIVER STATISTICS

Blaney continued to progress in 2002—albeit slowly. He is still waiting for his first Winston Cup victory and his first top-five finish but he recorded five top-10s and 20 top-20s.

DRIVER BIO	
Birth date:	**October 24, 1962**
Birthplace:	**Sharon, PA**
Team:	**Jasper Motorsports**
Sponsor:	**Jasper Engines and Transmissions**
Owner:	**Doug Bawel**
Crew Chief:	**Ryan Pemberton**
Car:	**Ford Taurus**

CAREER RECORD	
Rookie Year:	**2000**
Starts:	**111**
Wins:	**0**
Top 5s:	**0**
Top 10s:	**13**
Money:	**$5,994,965**
Highlights:	**Sprint Car Driver of the Year 1995.**

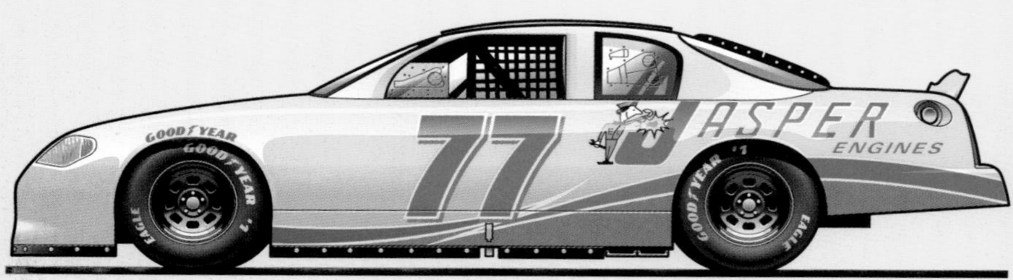

ABOVE RIGHT: Blaney's best finish was at Phoenix in November, where he came home seventh.

BELOW: Jasper Motorsports took some good results in 2002 despite a tight budget.

Impressive performances from sprint convert catch the eye.

Dave Blaney and the No. 77 Jasper Engines & Transmissions team have been asked to do a lot with a little. Hardly the most well-financed operation, the Jasper team overachieved in 2002, given the limited nature of its resources.

A lot of Jasper's success had to do with the 40-year-old Blaney, who appears to be coming into his own as a stock car driver. Blaney has a history of success in sprint cars—he was World of Outlaws champion and Sprint Car Driver of the Year in 1995—but before he signed on to drive Winston Cup cars for Bill Davis in 1999, his stock car experience was limited, to say the least.

After finishing 22nd in the Winston Cup standings in 2001, Blaney left Davis to take Robert Pressley's place in the No. 77. Though Blaney's performance wasn't exactly spectacular, his year was characterized by a number of extremely solid runs and consistent top-20 finishes. After Rockingham, Blaney was in the top 20 in six of the next seven races, and he posted his first top-10 of the year with a ninth at California, where he led 27 laps. Blaney qualified third for the September race at Richmond and matched his best finish to that point with another ninth.

As he matures as a stock car driver, his results will improve. One of his major assets is his working relationship with crew chief Ryan Pemberton, whose ingenuity has helped the Jasper team get the most from its cars.

Joe Gibbs Racing

ABOVE: For Tony Stewart's pit crew, the 2002 campaign ended in triumph as the No. 20 Home Depot Chevy won the championship.

Joe Gibbs once again shows the Midas touch as driver Tony Stewart hands the owner his second championship in three years.

Obviously, Joe Gibbs knows what it takes to build a championship organization. "Coach" took the NFL Washington Redskins to three Super Bowl titles before putting together a two-car race team that brought a Winston Cup championship to Bobby Labonte in 2000. In 2002, it was Tony Stewart's turn to make a successful championship run. Perhaps the most difficult task facing the strait-laced Gibbs is blending the combination of assertive and low-key personalities that work together in his operation. Though his accomplishments on the track were special, Stewart also attracted attention for his occasional outburst of temper. Crew chief Greg Zipadelli is a calming influence on the volatile driver.

Labonte and Jimmy Makar had the longest-lasting driver/crew chief relationship in the Winston Cup garage, but that bond didn't survive a season of frustration and disappointment in 2002. With Makar moving "upstairs" in his team manager's role, Michael "Fatback" McSwain will be calling the shots in the pits. Both Labonte and Makar are relatively laid back. McSwain, on the other hand, has a dominant personality. How the relationships between Labonte, Makar and McSwain develop will be a key to the No. 18's success in 2003. Comparatively, Gibbs' switch from Pontiac to Chevrolet shouldn't present any major obstacles.

TEAM STATISTICS

TEAM OWNER: JOE GIBBS

BOBBY LABONTE	
Driver Number:	**No. 18**
Crew Chief:	**Michael McSwain**
Team Sponsor:	**Interstate Batteries**

TONY STEWART	
Driver Number:	**No. 20**
Crew Chief:	**Greg Zipadelli**
Team Sponsor:	**Home Depot**

Bobby Labonte

18

Team and driver fail to gel, but Bobby still continues to win.

There's one consolation Bobby Labonte can derive from the 2002 Winston Cup season: he extended his streak of consecutive years with at least one victory to eight.

He ensured the continuation of that string with a dominating win at Martinsville on April 14, but that was the clear highlight of an otherwise undistinguished (and sometimes surprising) season.

In 2002, he opened the season with a 34th-place result in the Daytona 500. From that point on, things didn't get much better. Despite the victory at Martinsville, Labonte spent most of the year languishing between 17th and 20th in the standings. The lack of performance brought a shocking announcement: that Jimmy Makar, who had been with Labonte ever since he signed to drive for the Joe Gibbs-owned team before the 1995 season, would step down as crew chief. Though Makar will remain with Gibbs as general manager, the move brought an end to one of the tightest driver/crew relationships in the Winston Cup garage.

More shocking was the hiring of Michael "Fatback" McSwain to replace Makar. In an unexpected move, McSwain sought a release from his contract with Yates and signed on with Labonte. At first glance, the driver and his new crew chief seem an odd combination. How well the soft-spoken Labonte and the volatile McSwain work together will go a long way toward determing how the team will fare in 2003, when the Gibbs organization switches from Pontiac to Chevrolet.

ABOVE: The failure to produce a regular race-winning car led to the departure of crew chief Makar.

BELOW LEFT: The 2002 season was a huge struggle for the former champion.

DRIVER STATISTICS

Labonte finished 16th in the 2002 points standings, recording one victory, five top-fives and seven top-10s. He starts 2003 with both a new car and a new crew chief.

DRIVER BIO

Birth date:	**May 8, 1964**
Birthplace:	**Corpus Christi, TX**
Team:	**Joe Gibbs Racing**
Sponsor:	**Interstate Batteries**
Owner:	**Joe Gibbs**
Crew Chief:	**Michael McSwain**
Car:	**Chevrolet Monte Carlo**

CAREER RECORD

Rookie Year:	**1993**
Starts:	**745**
Wins:	**22**
Top 5s:	**181**
Top 10s:	**344**
Money:	**$29,804,794**
Highlights:	**Winston Cup champion 2000. Busch Series champion 1991.**

tony Stewart

20

DRIVER STATISTICS

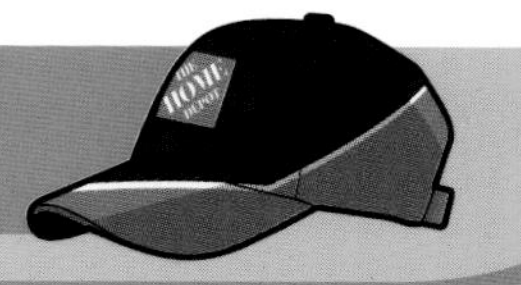

Despite six DNFs—the most of any of the top-10 drivers—Stewart was crowned champion. Alongside his three victories in 2002, he also posted 15 top-fives and 21 top-10s.

DRIVER BIO	
Birth date:	May 20, 1971
Birthplace:	Columbus, IN
Team:	Joe Gibbs Racing
Sponsor:	Home Depot
Owner:	Joe Gibbs
Crew Chief:	Greg Zipadelli
Car:	Chevrolet Monte Carlo

CAREER RECORD	
Rookie Year:	1999
Starts:	406
Wins:	15
Top 5s:	54
Top 10s:	86
Money:	$16,469,100
Highlights:	Winston Cup Champion 2002. Winston Cup Rookie of the Year 1999.

ABOVE: The outspoken Stewart has his detractors but his talents behind the wheel are undeniable.

BELOW: The No. 20 Pontiac rebounded from a poor start to finish at the top in 2002.

Stewart is crowned champion on the final day of the season.

Throughout his championship run in 2002, Tony Stewart seemed to be in the headlines—almost as often for his off-track outbursts as for his on-track accomplishments. But the volatile Stewart ultimately secured a Winston Cup title that for much of the season seemed there for the taking. The conventional wisdom says that championships are won with consistent performance throughout the season. Stewart defied that axiom. Though he was consistent enough when the No. 20 Pontiac was running at the end of a race (he led the series with 15 top-five finishes), Stewart fell out of six events—an extraordinarily high number of DNFs for an eventual champion.

In fact, the 31-year-old driver was dead last in the season opener at Daytona, where an engine failure on the third lap ended his race. A mere four races later, after a victory at Atlanta, Stewart had skyrocketed to fifth in the standings. He fell back to 10th after consecutive 29th-place results at Talladega and California, but his second victory of the season a week later—at Richmond—propelled Stewart toward the top of the standings.

After his third win of the season, at Watkins Glen, Stewart was fourth. A second-place finish at Talladega on Oct. 6, on a day that saw contenders Mark Martin and Jimmie Johnson both experience major problems, gave Stewart the points lead for the first time. Though he experienced some uneasy moments in the final race of the season at Homestead-Miami, Stewart never relinquished the top spot once he had gained it. He entered the season's final race with an 89-point lead over Martin, the only driver who could overtake him for the title at that point. Though Martin finished fourth, Stewart's 18th-place finish was enough to secure his first championship by 38 points.

Stewart's talent is undeniable, and he doubtless will mount a ferocious defense in 2003. But a larger question remains: how will the mercurial Stewart represent the sport that has crowned him champion?

MBV Motorsports

ABOVE: Veteran crew chief James Ince worked well with driver Johnny Benson, and their partnership became a winner late in the year.

Hard work and stability pay off for NASCAR's top singleton team with a winning day at Rockingham.

In a season where drivers, crew chiefs and car makes changed as quickly as the autumn leaves, the MBV Motorsports team was a study in stability.

Even before Benson won the first race of his Winston Cup career at Rockingham in November, he and crew chief James Ince had signed contract extensions that reportedly would keep them with owner Nelson Bowers through the 2004 season.

The 32-year-old Ince is a veteran who began his Winston Cup career turning wrenches for Ted Musgrave at Roush Racing. Like Benson, Ince earned his first victory in NASCAR's top series when his driver took the checkered flag at Rockingham.

Single-car operations are at a decided disadvantage because testing opportunities are limited, but if any solo team can succeed, MBV has an excellent chance. Ince and Benson seem a perfect match, and they will run their fourth full season together in 2003.

Benson missed five races because of cracked ribs in 2002 but still managed a respectable points finish, thanks to a late-season rally that included a second-place finish at Martinsville and the win at Rockingham. With a healthy Benson behind the wheel, this team could challenge the multi-car juggernauts in 2003.

TEAM STATISTICS

TEAM OWNER: JAMES ROCCO

JOHNNY BENSON	
Driver Number:	**No. 10**
Crew Chief:	**James Ince**
Team Sponsor:	**Valvoline**

Johnny Benson

10

Benson happy to shed "best driver never to win" tag.

When Johnny Benson needed to boost his spirits, he looked at Michael Waltrip's Winston Cup record. It took Waltrip 463 starts to win his first points race in NASCAR's top series. Benson, who inherited the designation "best driver never to have won," wasn't close to that milestone. But as the 2002 season progressed, he moved closer to Waltrip's colossal number.

It didn't help that Benson cracked his ninth rib on race weekend at Richmond in May. The 1995 Busch Series champion was making a rare start in the NASCAR's junior circuit, and it proved costly. On lap 21 a hard crash caused the injury that sidelined the 39-year-old Michigan driver for the next three Winston Cup events—at Richmond, Charlotte and Dover.

Benson returned to post a sixth-place finish at Michigan, but his comeback was cut short early in the Pepsi 400 at Daytona, where he hit the wall on lap 10 after contact with Waltrip—and cracked two ribs. Sidelined for the Cup races at Chicago and New Hampshire, Benson returned for the second time at Pocono in July and finished 30th.

During the latter half of the season, Benson appeared to shake off the effects of his injuries. He was eighth at Michigan, 12th at Bristol, fourth at New Hampshire, 10th at Dover, and second at Martinsville, as he steadily improved his points position from a season-worst 37th after missing the July race at New Hampshire.

On November 3 at North Carolina Speedway, in his 226rd Winston Cup start, Benson held off a charging Mark Martin over the final 12 laps of the Pop Secret Popcorn 400 to finally achieve his first Winston Cup victory. The sense of relief was obvious for the Michigan native.

If Benson can stay healthy in 2003, he stands a good chance of improving on his career-best 11th-place points finish, a mark he achieved in 1997 and 2001. Benson has a strong working relationship with crew chief James Ince, and his MBV Motorsports team got a head start on the 2003 season as part of the development effort for the new Pontiac.

ABOVE: The No. 10 Pontiac came on strong in the final third of the year.

BELOW LEFT: The popular Benson kept on smiling despite two rib-breaking crashes.

DRIVER STATISTICS

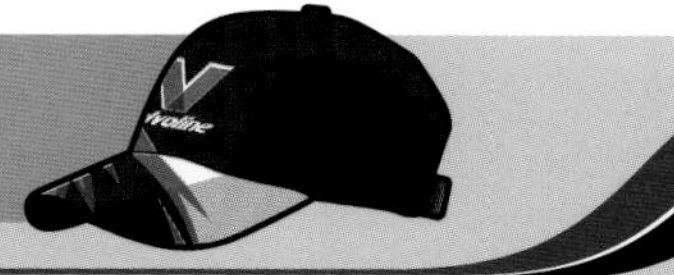

Benson finally broke through in 2002 recording his first Winston Cup victory. He also added three top-fives, seven top-10s and 16 top-20s, finishing 29th in the points standings.

DRIVER BIO

Birth date:	**June 27, 1963**
Birthplace:	**Grand Rapids, MI**
Team:	**MBV Motorsports**
Sponsor:	**Valvoline**
Owner:	**James Rocco**
Crew Chief:	**James Ince**
Car:	**Pontiac**

CAREER RECORD

Rookie Year:	**1996**
Starts:	**228**
Wins:	**1**
Top 5s:	**16**
Top 10s:	**54**
Money:	**$12,614,437**
Highlights:	**First Winston Cup win in 2002. Winston Cup Rookie of the Year 1996.**

Morgan-McClure Motorsports

ABOVE: For the 2003 Winston Cup series, Morgan-McClure Motorsports will replace the Chevy Monte Carlo with Pontiac, in hopes of improved performance.

For Morgan-McClure Motorsports a trip to Victory Lane in 2003 would be most welcome after another fruitless campaign in 2002.

At the height of its prowess in the mid-1990s, Morgan-McClure Motorsports was a dominant force on the restrictor-plate superspeedways of Daytona and Talladega. In fact, Sterling Marlin won back-to-back Daytona 500s for owner Larry McClure in 1994 and 1995. Between Ernie Irvan, whose seven races for MMM from 1990–1993 and Marlin, who garnered six wins during his 1994–1997 tenure, Morgan-McClure claimed 13 of its 14 victories as a race team.

Bobby Hamilton was responsible for MMM's other win—at Martinsville in 1998—but the organization hasn't visited Victory Lane since then. Current driver Mike Skinner, who moved from Richard Childress Racing to start the 2002, is winless in six full seasons as a Winston Cup driver. In those six seasons with Childress, Skinner made 10 front-row starts, including five from the pole.

Skinner started the 2002 season with Scott Eggleston as crew chief, but after a disappointing first half, Chris Carrier took Eggleston's place in June. But after the change, Skinner actually lost positions in the final Winston Cup standings. The team does have stability in its sponsorship. Kodak has been with Morgan-McClure since 1986, the longest-running continuous primary sponsorship in the series. A long-time Chevrolet team, MMM will try to improve its fortunes with a switch to Pontiac.

TEAM STATISTICS

TEAM OWNER: LARRY MCCLURE

MIKE SKINNER	
Driver Number:	**No. 4**
Crew Chief:	**Scott Eggleston**
Team Sponsor:	**Kodak**

Mike Skinner

DRIVER STATISTICS

The 2002 Winston Cup Series finished with Skinner still winless. He recorded just one top-10 and finished outside the top-30 in the final points standings.

DRIVER BIO	
Birth date:	**June 28, 1957**
Birthplace:	**Ontario, CA**
Team:	**Morgan McClure Motorsports**
Sponsor:	**Kodak**
Owner:	**Larry McClure**
Crew Chief:	**Scott Eggleston**
Car:	**Chevrolet Monte Carlo**

CAREER RECORD	
Rookie Year:	**1997**
Starts:	**203**
Wins:	**0**
Top 5s:	**10**
Top 10s:	**39**
Money:	**$11,249,698**
Highlights:	**Winston Cup Rookie of the Year 1997. Craftsmen Truck champion 1995.**

The 2002 campaign proved trying for Skinner as the wins refused to materialize. He will be hoping 2003 is the year of his breakthrough.

Despite a switch from Richard Childress Racing to Morgan-McClure Motorsports, Mike Skinner ended the 2002 season in the same position he started it—still looking for his first Winston Cup victory.

It was Skinner, you'll recall, who signed on with Childress in 1996 as a teammate to the late Dale Earnhardt. But in relation to the seven-time Winston Cup champion, Skinner was second banana in a two-banana bunch. His best finish with Childress was 10th in points in 1999, the same year he posted a career-best five top-five results.

The new alliance with Morgan-McClure failed to produce the desired results during Skinner's first year with the team. It wasn't until the 34th race of the 2002 season that Skinner posted his first top-10, a sixth at Rockingham. In the four restrictor-plate races, Skinner finished 23rd twice, 37th and 28th. And after climbing as high as 10th in points with Childress, Skinner spent his first season driving for Larry McClure unable to crack the top 25.

Skinner has talent. He proved that in the Craftsman Truck Series when he won the championship in 1995. But he has yet to prove himself at NASCAR's highest level. The problem isn't a lack of resources—the team has enjoyed backing from Kodak since 1986, the longest continuous primary sponsorship currently in the Winston Cup Series.

Realistically, a lack of team cohesion has to be at the root of a season that produced only one finish better than 20th in the first 15 races. A mid-season crew chief change from Scott Eggleston to Chris Carrier was designed to shake things up, but the move didn't seem to make a significant difference.

The entire organization has much to prove in 2003, but it's growing increasingly difficult for a single-car operation to remain competitive. For Skinner and Morgan-McClure, the coming season will be an uphill battle.

ABOVE RIGHT: The 45-year-old Skinner must be wondering if time is running out to make Victory Lane.

BELOW LEFT: The Kodak Chevy was well off the front-running pace all year.

Penske Racing South

Rookie Newman provides season highlight for Penske in 2002.

Though both of Roger Penske's drivers finished in the top 10 in points, the 2002 season was one of good news and bad news for the Mooresville, N.C.-based race team.

First the bad news: Rusty Wallace finished a frustrating year without a Winston Cup victory, the first time in 17 seasons he had finished a season without a trip to Victory Lane. The driver of the No. 2 Miller Lite car finished second three times: in the Pepsi 400 at Daytona, in the Brickyard 400 and in the Sharpie 500 at Bristol (after a bump-and-run from Jeff Gordon). With sprint car driver and former front-tire changer Bill Wilburn as his first-year crew chief, Wallace did qualify for the 2003 Bud Shootout with a pole at Dover.

Now, the good news: Ryan Newman saved the Penske honor with a victory at New Hampshire and battled Jimmie Johnson all season long for the Winston Cup rookie-of-the-year title. Newman finished sixth overall in the final standings, trailing fifth-place Johnson by seven points. Newman and crew chief Matt Borland have developed an extremely tight relationship—together they won a series-high six poles in 2002. And best of all, Newman just edged Johnson for the rookie-of-the-year honors.

The major change coming for the Penske teams in 2003 will be a switch from Ford to Dodge. And Wallace, a fiery veteran at 46, may have to get used to running behind his 25-year-old teammate.

TEAM STATISTICS

TEAM OWNER: ROGER PENSKE

RYAN NEWMAN	
Driver Number:	No. 12
Crew Chief:	Matt Borland
Team Sponsor:	Alltel/Mobil 1

RUSTY WALLACE	
Driver Number:	No. 2
Crew Chief:	Bill Wilburn
Team Sponsor:	Miller Lite

ABOVE: The Alltel/Mobil pit crew helped Ryan Newman to 2002 Rookie of the Year honors.

Ryan Newman

12

An awesome 2002 puts Newman in the limelight for 2003.

Ryan Newman is a gearhead. The 2002 Winston Cup rookie of the year has an engineering degree from Purdue University and an undeniable gift for driving a racecar. Matt Borland, crew chief for Newman's No. 12 Alltel car, approaches stock car racing from a high-tech perspective, as does Newman. So attuned are they to the handling characteristics of the car that it often seems that they are functioning as two parts of the same brain.

How else can one explain Newman's phenomenal success in 2002? After threatening to win a race for most of the season, he finally took the checkered flag at New Hampshire in September—but that was only a small part of what Newman accomplished. Not only did Newman win more poles than any other competitor in the series with six, but he also scored 14 top-five finishes, second only to series champion Tony Stewart's 15. Newman tied Winston Cup runner-up Mark Martin for most top-10s with 22.

And Newman's effort grew stronger as the season progressed. Twelfth in points after finishing 36th at Bristol in August, Newman began a steady climb through the standings. A second in the Southern 500 at Darlington, followed by a second at Richmond, after his victory at Loudon carried him to eighth. After four more top-10s in the next four weeks, including another second at Kansas City, Newman was fourth in the standings. Ultimately, he would finish sixth in Winston Cup points and win the rookie title by the narrowest of margins over Jimmie Johnson.

Newman and Borland exhibited their versatility with pole wins at a variety of different tracks: California, Chicagoland, New Hampshire, Martinsville, Rockingham and Phoenix. With such mastery of the qualifying process, and the proven ability to finish consistently in the top 10, Newman should be considered a Winston Cup title favorite in 2003. In fact, were it not for three engine failures and an overheating problem during a stretch of seven races in the spring, he might already be champion.

ABOVE: Newman ran well at a variety of tracks—a key to his rookie success.

BELOW: The cerebal Newman found the perfect crew chief in Matt Borland.

DRIVER STATISTICS

Newman was a consistant performer in 2002, racking up one win, 14 top-fives, 22 top-10s and 26 top-20s on his way to the coveted Rookie of the Year honors.

DRIVER BIO

Birth date:	**December 8, 1977**
Birthplace:	**South Bend, IN**
Team:	**Penske Racing**
Sponsor:	**Alltel/Mobil 1**
Owner:	**Roger Penske**
Crew Chief:	**Matt Borland**
Car:	**Ford Taurus**

CAREER RECORD

Rookie Year:	**2002**
Starts:	**44**
Wins:	**1**
Top 5s:	**16**
Top 10s:	**24**
Money:	**$4,876,931**
Highlights:	**Winston Cup Rookie of the Year 2002.**

Rusty Wallace

2

DRIVER STATISTICS

Wallace was without a victory in 2002—his first winless Winston Cup season. However, he still finished seventh in the points standings with seven top-5s and 17 top-10s.

DRIVER BIO	
Birth date:	**August 14, 1956**
Birthplace:	**Lake Norman, NC**
Team:	**Penske Racing**
Sponsor:	**Miller Lite**
Owner:	**Roger Penske**
Crew Chief:	**Bill Wilburn**
Car:	**Ford Taurus**

CAREER RECORD	
Rookie Year:	**1984**
Starts:	**598**
Wins:	**54**
Top 5s:	**218**
Top 10s:	**309**
Money:	**$33,737,234**
Highlights:	**Winston Cup champion 1989. Winston Cup Rookie of the year 1984.**

So near and yet so far for the winless Wallace in 2002.

Though Rusty Wallace stayed within sight of the Winston Cup points lead throughout much of the season, 2002 was a year of frustration for the 1989 champion. Wallace, like Jeff Gordon, couldn't seem to buy a victory. He hadn't won since April of 2001, and was just as hungry as Gordon when the Winston Cup Series visited Bristol in August. The Sharpie 500 at Thunder Valley was Wallace's best chance to end the dry spell, but Gordon bumped him out of the way in the closing laps to deprive the 46-year-old veteran of victory.

Despite failing to win, Wallace was fourth in the Winston Cup standings as late as July 21, when he started third and finished fourth in the New England 300 at New Hampshire.

On several occasions, Wallace came tantalizingly close to victory. He finished second in the Pepsi 400 at Daytona and was runner-up in the Brickyard 400 and in the shoot-out with Gordon at Bristol. But as fast and as consistent as Wallace was in 2002, there was always at least one driver who was faster. He nevertheless achieved a top-10 points finish with a first-year crew chief on the pit box. Bill Wilburn earned the promotion to crew chief when Robin Pemberton stepped back from an active role on Sundays before the season started.

Wilburn now has a full year's experience as the pit boss. That should facilitate Wallace's title run in 2003—if Wallace can beat young Penske Racing South teammate Ryan Newman to the checkered flag.

TOP ABOVE: Wallace's 17-year winning streak came to an abrupt end in 2002.

ABOVE: The Miller Lite Ford was a regular top-five challenger in 2002, but couldn't make Victory Lane.

Petty Enterprises

ABOVE: Kyle Petty and pit crew worked tirelessly throughout the 2002 Winston Cup season but couldn't find the results expected of the Petty name.

Hard work not enough to restore Petty to the top.

What will it take for the once-proud Petty organization to regain its former glory? This was the outfit founded by patriarch Lee Petty in 1949, NASCAR's first full year as a stock racing sanctioning body. This was the team that carried second-generation driver Richard Petty to a record seven Winston Cup championships. So why has Petty Enterprises been floundering for the better part of a decade?

Kyle Petty, who runs the organization and drives the No. 45 Dodge, hasn't found the answer to that question, though not for lack of trying. For that matter, Petty (at 22nd in points in 2002) posted his best finish since 1997, when he was 15th, but John Andretti suffered through a problem-filled season and finished 28th. Though Andretti was expected to drive the No. 43 Dodge in 2003, he had not signed a contract with Petty as of the season's final race.

Petty won his last Cup race in 1995 at Dover, and Andretti gave the Pettys their last victory at Phoenix in 1999. Petty Enterprises started the 2002 season as a three-car team, but Buckshot Jones was released after seven races and a motley crew of substitutes drove the No. 44 for the rest of the season. Open-wheeled racing star Christian Fittipaldi, who qualified for one Winston Cup event in 2002, will drive the No. 44 on a limited basis in 2003.

TEAM STATISTICS

TEAM OWNER: RICHARD PETTY

KYLE PETTY	
Driver Number:	**No. 45**
Crew Chief:	**Steve Lane**
Team Sponsor:	**Georgia Pacific**

JOHN ANDRETTI	
Driver Number:	**No. 43**
Crew Chief:	**Brandon Thomas**
Team Sponsor:	**Betty Crocker**

CHRISTIAN FITTIPALDI	
Driver Number:	**No. 44**
Crew Chief:	**Gary Putnam**
Team Sponsor:	**n/a**

Kyle Petty

ABOVE: The No. 45 Dodge needs to show more pace to go with its consistency.

BELOW RIGHT: For an eight-time race winner, struggling to make the top-10 is tough.

Petty will look to turn reliability into wins in 2003.

Considering his start to the 2002 season, Kyle Petty didn't have a bad year. On the other hand, the once-proud Petty dynasty didn't have a particularly good year either.

Thanks to an engine failure on lap 146 of the season-opening Daytona 500, Petty finished 41st. After a 37th-place result at Rockingham a week later, the 42-year-old son of seven-time Winston Cup champion Richard Petty stood 42nd in the series points standings. But with a string of top-20 finishes as the season progressed, Petty began to climb through the rankings. His best result came at Talladega, where he came home 10th, and he was 12th at Bristol and Michigan, 13th at Charlotte and Pocono, 14th at Darlington and 15th at Las Vegas.

After his 24th-pace finish at Chicagoland Speedway on July 14, Petty was 18th in the points. Despite losing a few positions later in the season, he posted his best result since 1997. The improvement was significant, but not what long-time fans have come to expect from the Petty organization.

As a driver and as a person, Petty is unique among Winston Cup drivers. His complexity and sensitivity may prevent him from achieving the "tunnel vision" necessary to contend for the title. In 2002, Petty drove the No. 45 Dodge to honor the memory of his son Adam, who was killed in a Busch Series crash at New Hampshire. But he hasn't won a Winston Cup race since 1995. If he can find his way to Victory Lane in 2003, no victory would be more welcome to race fans and fellow competitors alike.

DRIVER STATISTICS

Petty finished outside the top-20 in the final points standings and had another winless season. He posted just one top-10 finish and will demand more of himself in 2003.

DRIVER BIO	
Birth date:	**June 2, 1960**
Birthplace:	**Randleman, NC**
Team:	**Petty Enterprises**
Sponsor:	**Sprint PCS**
Owner:	**Kyle Petty**
Crew Chief:	**Steven Lane**
Car:	**Dodge Intrepid**

CAREER RECORD	
Rookie Year:	**1980**
Starts:	**645**
Wins:	**8**
Top 5s:	**51**
Top 10s:	**168**
Money:	**$15,327,388**
Highlights:	**Career high two wins in 1992.**

PPi Motorsports

ABOVE: PPi Motorsports will switch from the Ford Taurus to the new Pontiac Grand Prix for the 2003 season.

PPi switches its hopes to Pontiac in the wake of the 2002 season.

Despite Ricky Craven's solid performance in a Ford Taurus in 2002, PPI Motorsports owner Cal Wells III will switch to the revamped Pontiac Grand Prix for the 2003 season.

After analyzing the car makes available for his third season as a Winston Cup owner, Wells concluded that the Pontiac offered the best chance for his single-car operation to make an assault on the top 10 in the series points standings.

There is ample reason to trust the owner's judgment. Wells himself was an off-road racer, and he has fielded successful teams in CART and Formula Atlantic, as well as in off-road racing. Craven gave the 47-year-old Wells his first Winston Cup victory at Martinsville in 2001, and the team has threatened to return to Victory Lane on numerous occasions since then.

Crew chief Mike Beam is one of the top pit bosses in the garage. During a career that started in 1981, Beam has worked with Kyle Petty, Michael Waltrip, Bill Elliott, Sterling Marlin and Elliott Sadler, among others. Beam's team won the pit crew championship in 1997, his last year with Bill Elliott.

All the pieces are in place for Craven to build on his success in 2003, and if Wells is right about the new Pontiac, the top 10 should be well within reach for the driver from Newburgh, Me.

TEAM STATISTICS

TEAM OWNER: CAL WELLS III

RICKY CRAVEN	
Driver Number:	**No. 32**
Crew Chief:	**Mike Beam**
Team Sponsor:	**Tide**

Ricky Craven

Craven appears to be approaching his best after another good year.

Talk about driving under a microscope. When Ricky Craven returned to competition late in 1998, he knew that every move he made on the track, every bobble, every minute error in judgment would be suspect.

Post-concussion syndrome, the lingering aftereffect of a practice crash Craven suffered at Texas in 1997, forced the 36-year-old driver out of action after the first four races of 1998. Craven returned to the series at New Hampshire in the fall, but after four starts, he resigned his position as a driver for Hendrick Motorsports.

It was a long way back for Craven, but he endured the scrutiny and persevered. In 1999, he ran 12 races for owner Scott Barbour and 12 for Hal Hicks, with nondescript results. In 16 races for Hicks in 2000, Craven again failed to post a top-10—but he was regaining confidence.

The following season brought the association that would change the direction of Craven's career. He signed with car owner Cal Wells III and won his first Winston Cup race. All told, Craven posted seven top-10 finishes in his first season with Wells and continued his solid performance in 2002. Top-10 finishes at Rockingham, Atlanta, Charlotte, Richmond, Dover and New Hampshire provided ample evidence that Craven is capable of running well at any sort of racetrack, and it should no longer come as a surprise when he is in contention for a victory.

As his pit stops evidenced in 2002, Craven has a quality crew, led by crafty Mike Beam. If Wells can keep the team intact and hungry, Craven could be a threat to win every time he fires up the ignition in 2003.

ABOVE: Craven was equally at home on both short tracks and superspeedways in 2002.

BELOW LEFT: The Maine native will no doubt be in contention throughout the 2003 season.

DRIVER STATISTICS

Sadler's 2002 started off well, with all three of his top-five finishes coming in the first five races. A further six top-ten finishes put him well up in the points standings.

DRIVER BIO	
Birth date:	**May 24, 1966**
Birthplace:	**Bangor, ME**
Team:	**PPi Motorsports**
Sponsor:	**Tide**
Owner:	**Cal Wells III**
Crew Chief:	**Mike Beam**
Car:	**Pontiac Grand Prix**

CAREER RECORD	
Rookie Year:	**1995**
Starts:	**216**
Wins:	**1**
Top 5s:	**14**
Top 10s:	**33**
Money:	**$9,311,286**
Highlights:	**Rookie of the Year 1995. First Winston Cup win at Martinsville in 2001.**

Richard Childress Racing

ABOVE: Owner Richard Childress (right) will surely have many more triumphant Sundays in 2003 with the talented Kevin Harvick (middle) at the wheel.

A year without controversy would be a welcome sight in 2003.

When Richard Childress isn't happy, things change. That point was underlined in late May of 2002, when Childress attempted to jump-start his No. 29 and No. 31 teams with a wholesale change of crew chiefs and pit crews. In the Winston Cup Series' version of "Trading Places," Robby Gordon's crew chief, Gil Martin, moved to the No. 29 Chevy of Kevin Harvick, and Kevin Hamlin left Harvick to turn the wrenches for Gordon.

The shake-up helped, but it failed to produce the kind of results Childress wanted. On the eve of the season's final race at Homestead-Miami, Childress promised additional personnel changes for 2003. Most of the talk centered on the team of Jeff Green and crew chief Todd Berrier, though Green ended the year 17th in points, ahead of both Gordon (20th) and Harvick (21st). Collectively, though, that sort of middle-of-the-pack finish won't satisfy Childress, who was as close as anyone to a permanent resident of the head table in New York during his championship seasons with the late Dale Earnhardt.

One of Childress' major challenges of 2003 will be riding herd on the diverse personalities that inhabit his race shops, notably drivers Harvick and Gordon. Both have experienced more than their share of controversy in the past, but if anyone deserves the respect of those two strong-willed competitors, Childress is the man.

TEAM STATISTICS

TEAM OWNER: RICHARD CHILDRESS

KEVIN HARVICK	
Driver Number:	**No. 29**
Crew Chief:	**Gil Martin**
Team Sponsor:	**Goodwrench Service**

ROBBY GORDON	
Driver Number:	**No. 31**
Crew Chief:	**Kevin Hamlin**
Team Sponsor:	**Cingular Wireless**

JEFF GREEN	
Driver Number:	**No. 30**
Crew Chief:	**Todd Berrier**
Team Sponsor:	**America Online**

Kevin Harvick

DRIVER STATISTICS

Many impressive rookies struggle to make good their early promise, but Harvick's one victory, five top-fives and eight top-10s in 2002 was a solid, if below expectation, return.

DRIVER BIO	
Birth date:	**December 8, 1975**
Birthplace:	**Bakersfield, CA**
Team:	**Richard Childress Racing**
Sponsor:	**GM Goodwrench Service**
Owner:	**Richard Childress**
Crew Chief:	**Gil Martin**
Car:	**Chevrolet Monte Carlo**

CAREER RECORD	
Rookie Year:	**2001**
Starts:	**70**
Wins:	**3**
Top 5s:	**11**
Top 10s:	**24**
Money:	**$8,050,302**
Highlights:	**Rookie of the Year 2001. Busch Series champion 2001.**

ABOVE: Harvick's No. 29 Chevy in full flow is one of NASCAR's most thrilling sights.

TOP RIGHT: Controlling his emotions will be the key to success for Harvick in 2003.

A more mature Harvick points to a championship run in 2003.

After a magical rookie season, Kevin Harvick's Winston Cup career hit a king-sized speed bump in 2002.

The 2001 Rookie of the Year's sophomore season started inauspiciously—and went from bad to worse. He started second for his first Daytona 500 and led three laps, but a wreck relegated him to a 36th-place finish. The driver nicknamed "Happy" was anything but, when an altercation with Greg Biffle after a Craftsman Truck Series at Bristol cost him a $15,000 fine and five months' probation. But Harvick's exploits in the Truck Series weren't over. NASCAR slapped him with a $35,000 fine, extended his probation through the end of the year and parked him for the Winston Cup race at Martinsville for on-track incidents involving Truck Series driver Coy Gibbs.

Harvick's fortunes did improve a little. For the second year in a row he won at Chicago in July, and that victory started a stretch of six top-10 finishes in seven races.

With the turmoil of 2002 behind him, Harvick could be a championship contender in 2003, if he can keep his emotions under control. Harvick is a racer who likes to compete as often as possible. With probation looming over him, Harvick curtailed his activities in the Truck and Busch Series in 2002. This year will be a different story. With Childress' blessing, Harvick plans to compete as often as his schedule will allow—and his performance should be the better for it.

Robby Gordon

31

Several impressive performances in the latter half of the 2002 season give Gordon a reason to be confident entering the new year.

With his first Winston Cup victory at New Hampshire in November of 2001, Robby Gordon raised expectations for the 2002 season, but the results were slow in coming.

The end of May arrived, and Gordon had yet to score a top-10 finish. His teammate, Kevin Harvick, was struggling, too. Consequently, team owner Richard Childress agreed to a radical move—a "swap" of crew chiefs that would bring most of Harvick's team to Gordon's pit and vice versa. Crew chief Gil Martin left to turn the wrenches for Harvick, and Kevin Hamlin took over the pit duties for Gordon.

The move, which took place in early June, had an immediate, positive effect. After an eighth-place finish at Dover, Gordon had a stretch of four mediocre results that prevented him from climbing higher than 26th in the points standings. But a five-race string that started with an eighth-place finish at Chicago improved his fortunes.

Gordon followed the Chicago race with a seventh at New Hampshire, a 25th at Pocono, an eighth at Indianapolis and a third on the road course at Watkins Glen. Gordon's rally in the second half of the season carried him as high as 19th in the series standings.

An experienced off-road and open-wheeled racer, Gordon is finally beginning to translate his talent into the stock car circuit. With a stable ownership situation and crew chief he can work with, Gordon could be a factor in the 2003 championship battle.

ABOVE: The second half of Gordon's season showed the true potential of the No. 31 Chevy.

BELOW: Another Winston Cup victory will be Gordon's main aim in 2003.

DRIVER STATISTICS

In 2002, Gordon took just one top-five and five top-10s on his way to 20th in the points, earning $3,054,240 in the process.

DRIVER BIO	
Birth date:	**January 2, 1969**
Birthplace:	**Cornelius, NC**
Team:	**Richard Childress Racing**
Sponsor:	**Cingular Wireless**
Owner:	**Richard Childress**
Crew Chief:	**Kevin Hamlin**
Car:	**Chevrolet Monte Carlo**

CAREER RECORD	
Rookie Year:	**1997**
Starts:	**98**
Wins:	**1**
Top 5s:	**5**
Top 10s:	**11**
Money:	**$5,570,385**
Highlights:	**First Winston Cup win at New Hampshire in 2001.**

Jeff Green

30

Often the forgotten man of the Richard Childress stable, Green's consistency in 2002 left him as the team's top gun.

Let's have a show of hands. Back in February, how many of you thought Jeff Green would be the leading driver for Richard Childress Racing at the end of the 2002 season?

Most of your money would have been on Kevin Harvick, who showed such promise during his 2001 rookie season. But Harvick's temper got him in trouble once too often, and NASCAR kept him on the sidelines for the spring race at Martinsville (and on probation for the the year).

Your second choice probably would have been Robby Gordon, who, like Harvick, notched his first Winston Cup victory in 2001. A hotshot in open-wheeled cars, Gordon is finally coming into his own in Winston Cup.

But when the tire smoke from the final "donut" had dissipated, the top dog in the Childress compound was Green, who "out-steadied" his more rambunctious teammates. Green wasn't spectacular, but his effort gained momentum as the season progressed. In the latter half, he began to add a few top-fives and top-10s to his customary middle-of-the-pack runs, and he achieved his successes on a variety of different racetracks.

Green was impressive in finishing fifth on Sonoma's road course in June. At New Hampshire in July, he was a strong second to Ward Burton on Loudon's one-mile flat track. For an encore, Green came home ninth at Michigan, third at Richmond and fifth at NASCAR's largest superspeedway, Talladega.

Young crew chief Todd Berrier and Green have developed a strong working relationship. It was Berrier, after all, who led Harvick's crew to the 2001 Busch Series title.

Green's brothers and fellow racers—David and Mark—have always maintained that Jeff is the best driver of the three. Now he's proving it, and the 2003 season should give him ample opportunity to showcase his talent.

ABOVE: A great relationship with crew cheif Todd Berrrier helped the No. 30 Chevy performances.
BELOW: Green may have a lower profile than his teammates but he lets his driving do the talking.

DRIVER STATISTICS

The 2002 season was an unsettled ride for Childress Racing but Green performed solidly, ending the year with a 17th place points finish, four top-fives and six top-10s.

DRIVER BIO	
Birth date:	**September 6, 1962**
Birthplace:	**Owensboro, KY**
Team:	**Richard Childress Racing**
Sponsor:	**AOL**
Owner:	**Richard Childress**
Crew Chief:	**Todd Berrier**
Car:	**Chevrolet Monte Carlo**

CAREER RECORD	
Rookie Year:	**1997**
Starts:	**94**
Wins:	**0**
Top 5s:	**5**
Top 10s:	**9**
Money:	**$3,731,861**
Highlights:	**Busch Series champion 2000. Won Bud Pole at Bristol in 2001.**

Robert Yates Racing

ABOVE: Dale Jarrett's pit crew celebrate another trip to Victory Lane but they will be looking for greater consistency in 2003.

Sadler joins the team for 2003 after Rudd's departure.

Dale Jarrett's new teammate, Elliott Sadler, will sport a new look for 2003. The No. 38 Ford will replace the No. 28 in the Robert Yates Racing shop, and M&M's will replace Texaco Havoline as the car's primary sponsor.

Perhaps the change is for the better. The No. 28 is associated with two drivers who are no longer living (Davey Allison, killed in a helicopter accident in 1993, and Kenny Irwin, who died in a practice crash at New Hampshire in 2000 after leaving the Yates ride in 1999). Ernie Irvan, driver of the No. 28 from 1993-1997, suffered critical injuries in a practice crash at Michigan in 1994.

Michael "Fatback" McSwain is slated to retain his role as crew chief. It was friction between McSwain and Ricky Rudd that contributed to Rudd's departure from the No. 28 at the end of the 2002 season. Communication between McSwain and Sadler will be critical to the team's success in 2003. McSwain insists he's looking forward to working with a young driver, and indeed, team chemistry will be crucial to Sadler's ability to realize his potential as a driver.

It's interesting to note that despite the turmoil at the No. 28 shop—which reached a low point when Rudd was sucker-punched by an employee at the Yates engine shop—Rudd and McSwain cooperated sufficiently to achieve a solid points finish. Now we'll see what happens if and when there's a harmonious atmosphere in the garage.

TEAM STATISTICS

TEAM OWNER: ROBERT YATES

DALE JARRETT	
Driver Number:	**No. 88**
Crew Chief:	**Todd Parrott**
Team Sponsor:	**UPS**

ELLIOTT SADLER	
Driver Number:	**No. 38**
Crew Chief:	**Michael McSwain**
Team Sponsor:	**M&M's**

dale jarrett

DRIVER STATISTICS

Despite scoring two victories, 10 top-fives and 18 top-10s, the 2002 Winston Cup season wasn't as Jarrett would have hoped for, as he settled for a ninth-place finish in the points standings.

DRIVER BIO	
Birth date:	**November 26, 1956**
Birthplace:	**Newton, NC**
Team:	**Robert Yates Racing**
Sponsor:	**UPS**
Owner:	**Robert Yates**
Crew Chief:	**Todd Parrott**
Car:	**Ford Taurus**

CAREER RECORD	
Rookie Year:	**1987**
Starts:	**495**
Wins:	**30**
Top 5s:	**177**
Top 10s:	**228**
Money:	**$37,210,502**
Highlights:	**Winston Cup champion 1999. Three-time Daytona 500 winner.**

Two wins were the highlight of an otherwise frustrating 2002.

Perhaps some of the turmoil on Ricky Rudd's side of the Robert Yates Racing garage spilled over into the Dale Jarrett team. Perhaps it was merely a star-crossed season in which circumstances conspired against the 1999 Winston Cup champion. Whatever the case, Jarrett struggled through a disappointing season in 2002. True, he had two victories by the middle of August—at Pocono and at Michigan—but a disastrous start to the season had already taken Jarrett out of the championship battle.

Jarrett finished 14th in the 2002 Daytona 500. In the second race of the season, at Rockingham, an engine failure dropped Jarrett to a 42nd-place finish. Three events later, another blown motor at Darlington dropped him to 21st in the points standings. He was 24th two weeks later after finishing 29th at Bristol and 24th at Texas.

It was at that point in the season that Jarrett began a steady climb back toward respectability. He finished fourth at Martinsville and backed that up with consecutive sixths at Talladega and California. In June, came the victory at Pocono and a second in the season's first race at Michigan. When the Winston Cup Series returned to Michigan in August, Jarrett qualified eighth and won the race.

Though Jarrett rallied for a decent points finish, neither he, crew chief Todd Parrott nor owner Robert Yates will be content with a "respectable" result. Expect better things from Jarrett in 2003.

ABOVE: Jarrett proved he still can drive with the best with wins at Pocono and Michigan.

TOP LEFT: Inconsistant performances plagued Jarrett in 2002 and left his title challenge cold.

Elliott Sadler

38

Salder will be looking for his team move to translate into wins.

The 2003 season presents a watershed opportunity to Elliott Sadler, who moves to Robert Yates Racing's No. 38 after three years with the Virginia-based Wood Brothers operation.

Sadler raised eyebrows in the spring of 2002 when he asked the Woods to release him from his contract at the end of the season. After Ricky Rudd's situation with Yates deteriorated beyond repair, Sadler was anointed in August as Yates' new driver for 2003. He'll team with 1999 Winston Cup champion Dale Jarrett in the two-car stable. Ironically, Rudd will take Sadler's place with his fellow Virginians, the Woods.

Sadler's 2002 seasons started strong—and quickly deteriorated. He finished second to Ward Burton in the season-opening Daytona 500, but consecutive 40th- and 39th-place finishes at Talladega and California, respectively, dropped Sadler to 25th in points by the end of April.

After requesting his release from the Wood Brothers, Sadler climbed as high as 18th in the points standings but the summer rally faded as fall approached.

Given that Sadler's first four years in Winston Cup produced but one victory (March 25, 2001 at Bristol), the move to Yates represents the chance to define his career.

"I had a lot of sleepless nights before I got this deal done," Sadler said of the agreement with Yates. "Now that it's done, I think I'm sleeping worse, because now it's a lot of pressure to get in this race car next year. I need to win races. We need to run good each and every week."

ABOVE: Sadler will swap the No. 21 Wood Brothers Ford for the Robert Yates No. 38 in 2003.

BELOW: Sadler will be hoping that a new team will bring him better fortunes.

DRIVER STATISTICS

Sadler failed to add to his victory total in 2002. He finished 23rd in the points standings, posting two top-fives, seven top-10s and 16 top-20s.

DRIVER BIO	
Birth date:	**April 30, 1975**
Birthplace:	**Emoria, VA**
Team:	**Robert Yates Racing**
Sponsor:	**M&M's**
Owner:	**Robert Yates**
Crew Chief:	**Michael McSwain**
Car:	**Ford Taurus**

CAREER RECORD	
Rookie Year:	**1999**
Starts:	**141**
Wins:	**1**
Top 5s:	**4**
Top 10s:	**11**
Money:	**$9,286,817**
Highlights:	**First Winston Cup victory at Bristol in 2001.**

Roush Racing

ABOVE: The No. 6 Viagra Ford helped Mark Martin to a run at the Winston Cup title in 2002.

TEAM STATISTICS

TEAM OWNER: JACK ROUSH

JEFF BURTON	
Driver Number:	**No. 99**
Crew Chief:	**Paul Andrews**
Team Sponsor:	**CITGO**
KURT BUSCH	
Driver Number:	**No. 97**
Crew Chief:	**Jimmy Fennig**
Team Sponsor:	**Rubbermaid**
MATT KENSETH	
Driver Number:	**No. 17**
Crew Chief:	**Robbie Reiser**
Team Sponsor:	**Dewalt**
MARK MARTIN	
Driver Number:	**No. 6**
Crew Chief:	**Ben Leslie**
Team Sponsor:	**Viagra**
GREG BIFFLE	
Driver Number:	**No. 16**
Crew Chief:	**Randy Goss**
Team Sponsor:	**Grainger**

Roush Racing in Victory Lane was a common sight in 2002.

Team owner Jack Roush will have quite the armada heading into the 2003 season. All told, Roush drivers posted 10 victories during the 2002 campaign, led by Matt Kenseth's series-best four. Not far behind was sophomore Winston Cup driver Kurt Busch, who totaled four wins, three in the last five races of the season.

The year was a vindication for Roush, who narrowly escaped death on his 60th birthday when the private plane he was piloting hit a power line and crashed. Roush teams had won only two races in 2001, but the 2002 season saw an invigorated operation and an invigorated Mark Martin, who finished second to Tony Stewart in the championship standings and silenced critics who had questioned his desire to compete. Joining Roush's potent Winston Cup roster in 2003 will be Busch Series champ Greg Biffle, who saw limited action in NASCAR's top series in 2002, driving for a variety of owners, including Roush, Kyle Petty and Andy Petree.

Roush's foremost challenge for 2003 is to return driver Jeff Burton to the ranks of championship contenders. Burton suffered through a winless season for the first time since 1996. In September, the team hired Paul Andrews to replace crew chief Frankie Stoddard, who was relieved of his duties, but the move failed to have a major positive effect on Burton's fortunes. With the entire off-season to prepare, however, Burton and Andrews make a formidable team for 2003.

Jeff Burton

DRIVER STATISTICS

Five top-fives and 14 top-10s earned Burton a solid 12th in the points in 2002, but he will expect to improve on that in 2003 and return to Victory Lane.

DRIVER BIO	
Birth date:	**June 29, 1967**
Birthplace:	**South Boston, VA**
Team:	**Roush Racing**
Sponsor:	**CITGO**
Owner:	**Jack Roush**
Crew Chief:	**Paul Andrews**
Car:	**Ford Taurus**

CAREER RECORD	
Rookie Year:	**1994**
Starts:	**295**
Wins:	**17**
Top 5s:	**86**
Top 10s:	**133**
Money:	**$26,821,719**
Highlights:	**Rookie of the Year 1994. Career-best third in points 2000.**

Even a new crew chief couldn't kick-start Burton in 2002.

After more than a year-and-a-half of inconsistent finishes, Jeff Burton could live with mediocrity no longer. Mired in 13th place in the standings after the Southern 500, Burton was in dire need of a kick-start. The answer was the unexpected release of crew chief Frankie Stoddard, who had led Burton's over-the-wall gang since 1998.

Team owner Jack Roush offered Stoddard a cosmetic move to the "front office," but Stoddard declined. Ultimately, the garrulous Stoddard accepted a job as crew chief for Burton's brother Ward for the remainder of the 2003 season. Roush hired well-traveled Paul Andrews, who served as crew chief for the late Alan Kulwicki during his 1992 championship season, to replace Stoddard.

But the change had relatively little immediate effect. Burton was third in points after a pair of top-10 finishes at Rockingham and Las Vegas but by the time an accident knocked him out of the April 7 race at Texas, he had slipped to 14th in the standings. He made a brief return to the top-10 after a third at Dover and a sixth at Pocono on consecutive weekends in June, but Burton lost ground during the next four events.

What does Burton need to return to form in 2003? It would help if his engine shop could eliminate the motor failures that cost him dearly in 2002. And Burton will have to improve his own qualifying efforts. His frequent inability to grab a starting spot near the front of the field often leaves him vulnerable to a mid-pack accident.

ABOVE: Burton will need to improve on his qualifying times in 2003.

TOP LEFT: The 2002 campaign was one of frustration for Burton.

Kurt Busch

97

Back-to-back wins indicate Busch's huge potential.

If the 2002 season produced a major surprise, Kurt Busch's performance certainly is strong candidate for that distinction.

The brash 24-year-old driver from Las Vegas, Nev., more than justified the decision of team owner Jack Roush to hire a young driver with such a limited background in stock cars. He earned a full-time promotion to Winston Cup for the 2001 season and his best finish that year was a third at Talladega—one of six top-10s for the rookie driver.

Busch's sophomore season saw his talent come to fruition. In March he scored his first Winston Cup victory at Bristol. In October he won for the second time at another of the Winston Cup circuit's traditional short tracks, Martinsville. One week later Busch won for the first time on a superspeedway, when he took the checkered flag at Atlanta. The back-to-back wins left Busch solidly in the top 10 in the points standings and put him in a position to contend for the series championship in 2003.

Though Busch has learned to control his No. 97 Sharpie Ford, he must also learn to control his emotions. Busch earned the reputation as a hothead after a collision with Jimmy Spencer knocked him out of the Brickyard 400 at Indianapolis.

In a fit of pique, Busch referred to Spencer as a "decrepit old has-been." But anyone who will be a serious challenger for the Winston Cup championship needs the respect and trust of his fellow drivers, and in some quarters, the jury is still out on the young star. Crew chief Jimmy Fennig needs to be a calming influence on his volatile driver.

ABOVE: Victories on both short tracks and superspeedways show Busch has no weakness.

BELOW LEFT: Busch may be a little arrogant for some but his talent is undeniable.

DRIVER STATISTICS

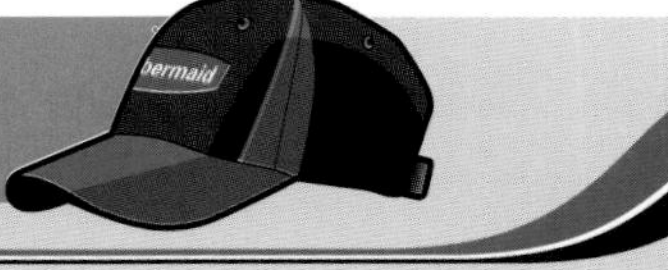

Busch was one of 2002's real stars. He visited Victory Lane four times, posted 12 top-fives, 20 top-10s and finished the year third in the overall points standings.

DRIVER BIO	
Birth date:	**August 9, 1978**
Birthplace:	**Las Vegas, NV**
Team:	**Roush Racing**
Sponsor:	**Rubbermaid**
Owner:	**Jack Roush**
Crew Chief:	**Jimmy Fennig**
Car:	**Ford Taurus**

CAREER RECORD	
Rookie Year:	**2001**
Starts:	**78**
Wins:	**4**
Top 5s:	**12**
Top 10s:	**20**
Money:	**$6,206,194**
Highlights:	**Won first Winston Cup race at Bristol in 2002.**

Matt Kenseth

Winning wasn't a problem for Kenseth in 2002.

The 2002 season was one of "might-have-beens" for Roush Racing driver Matt Kenseth.

After wrecking and finishing 33rd in the Daytona 500, the 30-year-old driver from Cambridge, Wis., began a meteoric rise through the Winston Cup Series points standings. A week after the disappointment at Daytona, he won the season's second race at Rockingham.

Two months later, Kenseth collected his second victory of the season at Texas, and in the next event, he was runner-up at Martinsville. A sixth-place result at Richmond in May boosted Kenseth to second in the points standings, a position he solidified with a second-place finish at Charlotte. Kenseth won the pole for the June race at Dover, but finished 40th and lost two positions in the points. A 35th-place result at Pocono one week later cost him three more places. Kenseth stopped the slide with his third win of the campaign in June at Michigan, but after three finishes of 30th or worse in the next four races, he found himself 10th in points.

Kenseth collected his fourth victory of the year at Richmond but an engine failure at Charlotte destroyed the last of his title hopes.

But for a few major setbacks, Kenseth might have won the championship in 2002. There's no denying his talent. In each of his three Winston Cup seasons, the laid-back driver has improved. Kenseth's crew chief, Robbie Reiser, was his car owner in the Busch Series, and the two have developed a long-standing relationship of mutual trust and respect. All signs point to Kenseth as a strong championship contender in 2003.

ABOVE: The No. 17 Ford was a regular visitor to Victory Lane in 2002.

BELOW: Greater consistency will see Kenseth challenge for the Winston Cup title in 2003.

DRIVER STATISTICS

The 2002 Winston Cup Series was a breakthrough for Kenseth as he finished the year with a season-high five victories. He also posted 11 top-fives and 19 top-10s.

DRIVER BIO

Birth date:	**April 10, 1972**
Birthplace:	**Cambridge, WI**
Team:	**Roush Racing**
Sponsor:	**DeWalt Power Tools**
Owner:	**Jack Roush**
Crew Chief:	**Robbie Reiser**
Car:	**Ford Taurus**

CAREER RECORD

Rookie Year:	**1993**
Starts:	**112**
Wins:	**6**
Top 5s:	**20**
Top 10s:	**41**
Money:	**$9,048,468**
Highlights:	**Rookie of the Year 2000. Busch Series runner-up in 1998.**

Mark Martin

DRIVER STATISTICS

Despite only recording a single victory in 2002, Martin made a run at the championship thanks to 12 top-fives, 22 top-tens and 28 top-20s.

DRIVER BIO	
Birth date:	**January 9, 1959**
Birthplace:	**Batesville, AR**
Team:	**Roush Racing**
Sponsor:	**Viagra**
Owner:	**Jack Roush**
Crew Chief:	**Ben Leslie**
Car:	**Ford Taurus**

CAREER RECORD	
Rookie Year:	**1982**
Starts:	**530**
Wins:	**33**
Top 5s:	**200**
Top 10s:	**314**
Money:	**$34,444,722**
Highlights:	**Three-time Winston Cup runner-up (2002, 1998, 1990).**

ABOVE: The veteran Martin will hope 2003 brings him his first title after four second-place finishes.
TOP RIGHT: The No. 6 Ford was a model of consistency in 2002.

Martin comes close to first Winston Cup title in 2002.

Though Mark Martin's most cherished goal continued to elude him, the 2002 season was a redemption of sorts for the 43-year-old driver from Batesville, Arkansas. Though the entire Roush Racing organization had suffered through a mediocre campaign in 2001, the brunt of the criticism fell on Martin, whose will to win was called into question. With the help of new crew chief Ben Leslie, Martin laid the doubts to rest in 2002 with a solid and intensely competitive effort that fell just short of a Winston Cup championship.

Martin was right in the mix throughout the entire season and his progression to the top of the standings seemed inexorable. He climbed to second in points in June, and for the second half of the season he stood no worse than third.

Though Martin scored only one victory during the season, his performance was so consistent that a Winston Cup title seemed well within his grasp. But circumstances conspired to deny Martin his first championship. An engine failure at Kansas City was followed a week later by a freak accident at Talladega when Martin's power steering went haywire on a pace lap. A 25-point penalty for an unapproved front spring kept him 89 points behind Tony Stewart entering the season's final race at Homestead-Miami. Martin finished fourth, though Stewart did enough to secure the championship. But Martin reestablished himself as a contender, and perhaps 2003 will finally mark his breakthrough season.

Wood brothers

ABOVE: After a tumultuous 2002 season, Rudd will step behind the wheel of the legendary No. 21 Wood Brothers Ford in 2003.

The hiring of Ricky Rudd points to an interesting season ahead.

With his move to Wood Brothers Racing in Stuart, Va., Ricky Rudd joins one of the most experienced, and historically, one of the most innovative teams in the Winston Cup garage. Brothers Glen and Leonard Wood have been fielding cars on NASCAR's elite circuit since 1953, and they have at least one victory to show for their efforts in five straight decades, including the current one.

After weathering a "lame-duck" season with Elliott Sadler behind the wheel (Sadler announced his desire to leave the team in the spring of 2002), the Woods have added Rudd's name to a Hall-of-Fame list of past drivers that includes Curtis Turner, David Pearson, Cale Yarborough, A.J. Foyt, Marvin Panch, Dan Gurney, Buddy Baker, Neil Bonnett, Kyle Petty and Dale Jarrett.

In Rudd, the Wood Brothers get a driver who started the 2002 season 24th on the all-time Winston Cup victory list with 22. In contrast, Sadler had a single win, notched when he took the checkered flag in the Woods' No. 21 at Bristol in March of 2001. Perhaps the Woods will provide the same sort of fountain of youth for Rudd that Bill Elliott discovered when he began his association with owner Ray Evernham.

Crew chief Pat Tryson should be a welcome change for Rudd, who suffered through a year of friction with Michael McSwain, his pit boss at Robert Yates Racing. Though the change of teams may mean a small sacrifice for Rudd in the caliber of the equipment he drives, his comfort level at the Wood Brothers' shop should increase exponentially. Whether that will be enough for Rudd and the Woods to contend for a championship remains to be seen.

TEAM STATISTICS

TEAM OWNERS: GLEN AND LEONARD WOOD

RICKY RUDD	
Driver Number:	**No. 21**
Crew Chief:	**Pat Tryson**
Team Sponsor:	**Motorcraft Quality Parts**

Ricky Rudd

21

After the troubles of 2002, Rudd finds a new home.

How do you spell relief? For Ricky Rudd the answer is "W-o-o-d B-r-o-t-h-e-r-s."

After a season of frustration and turmoil at Robert Yates Racing, the no-nonsense veteran has allied himself with his neighbors from Virginia for the 2003 campaign.

Simply put, Rudd and his crew chief at Yates Racing, Michael "Fatback" McSwain didn't get along. The rancor spread throughout the entire team—to the point that Yates' engine shop employee Larry Lackey took exception to some of Rudd's comments about his motor and punched Rudd after the September race at Richmond.

Rudd retaliated by throwing his water bottle at Lackey, and both were subsequently fined by NASCAR for conduct detrimental to racing. That, in microcosm, was the season for Rudd and the No. 28 Havoline Ford.

Though chaos was the dominant theme, there were happier moments for Rudd, who won at least one race per year from 1983 through 1998. One of Winston Cup's most proficient road-course racers, Rudd visited Victory Lane at Sonoma in June.

Rudd first raced in the Winston Cup Series in 1975. The Wood Brothers have fielded teams in NASCAR's foremost series since 1953. Perhaps the combination of a veteran driver and one of NASCAR's most venerated racing teams will prove a comfortable fit as the 46-year-old Rudd nears the end of his driving career.

ABOVE: Rudd will replace the No. 28 Havoline Ford with the No. 21 of the Wood Brothers.

BELOW: The veteran Rudd will hope for a more settled—and more productive—season in 2003.

DRIVER STATISTICS

Despite the turmoil in 2002, Rudd did manage to post a victory. He also recorded eight top-fives and 12 top-10s, finishing a respectable 10th in the final points standings.

DRIVER BIO	
Birth date:	September 12, 1956
Birthplace:	Chesapeake, VA
Team:	Wood Brothers Racing
Sponsor:	Motorcraft Quality Parts
Owner:	Glen and Leonard Wood
Crew Chief:	Pat Tryson
Car:	Ford Taurus

CAREER RECORD	
Rookie Year:	1977
Starts:	767
Wins:	23
Top 5s:	187
Top 10s:	356
Money:	$28,539,603
Highlights:	Rookie of the Year 1977. Winston Cup runner-up 1991.

Other teams and drivers

Greg Biffle. Brett Bodine.
Todd Bodine. Jamie McMurray.

A.J. Foyt Racing. Brett Bodine Racing.
Haas-Carter Motorsports.
MB2 Motorsports.

ABOVE: Jamie McMurray capitalized on Sterling Marlin's misfortune, driving the No. 40 Coors Light to victory in just his second ever Winston Cup start.

Greg Biffle

The 2002 Busch Series champion has limited Winston Cup experience but Roush will expect a solid rookie campaign.

So what else did Greg Biffle do in 2002, aside from winning the Busch Series championship? Biffle, who takes the wheel of Jack Roush's No. 16 Ford for the 2003 Winston Cup season, competed in seven Cup events in 2002, the maximum number allowed without compromising his rookie status for the 2003 campaign.

Interestingly enough, however, Biffle ran just one race in Roush's Ford. His other forays into the Winston Cup series came in substitute roles for other teams. He replaced injured Bobby Hamilton in Andy Petree's No. 55 Chevrolet four races late in the season. Biffle posted two excellent qualifying results in Hamilton's car (fourth at New Hampshire and fifth at Dover), but his best finish in a race for Petreee was 27th at New Hampshire. Biffle took the controls of the Petty organization's No. 44 Dodge for the November race at Rockingham, where he started 13th and finished 25th. After locking up the Busch Series championship, Biffle saw double duty at Homestead-Miami, where he competed in the final Cup race of the season, again in Petty's Dodge.

Biffle's finishes, however, weren't indicative of his talent. As a Busch Series rookie in 2001, he won five races. He was a star in the Craftsman Truck Series before moving to Busch, and in 2002, he gave Roush Racing its first championship in any one of NASCAR's top three series.

In 2003, Biffle will challenge the top drivers in NASCAR's elite division, he'll have the help of crew chief Randy Goss, who moves with his driver from the Busch Series, in doing so. Known as an aggressive driver with a willingness to trade paint with his fellow competitors, Biffle may have to tone his act down a bit during his rookie season in Winston Cup. On the other hand, Biffle's star hasn't been on the rise because he's bashful—in big-time stock car racing, the meek inherit nothing.

BELOW: Behind the wheel, Biffle is known for his aggressive approach, which helped him win the 2002 Busch Series Championship and makes him a driver to watch in 2003.

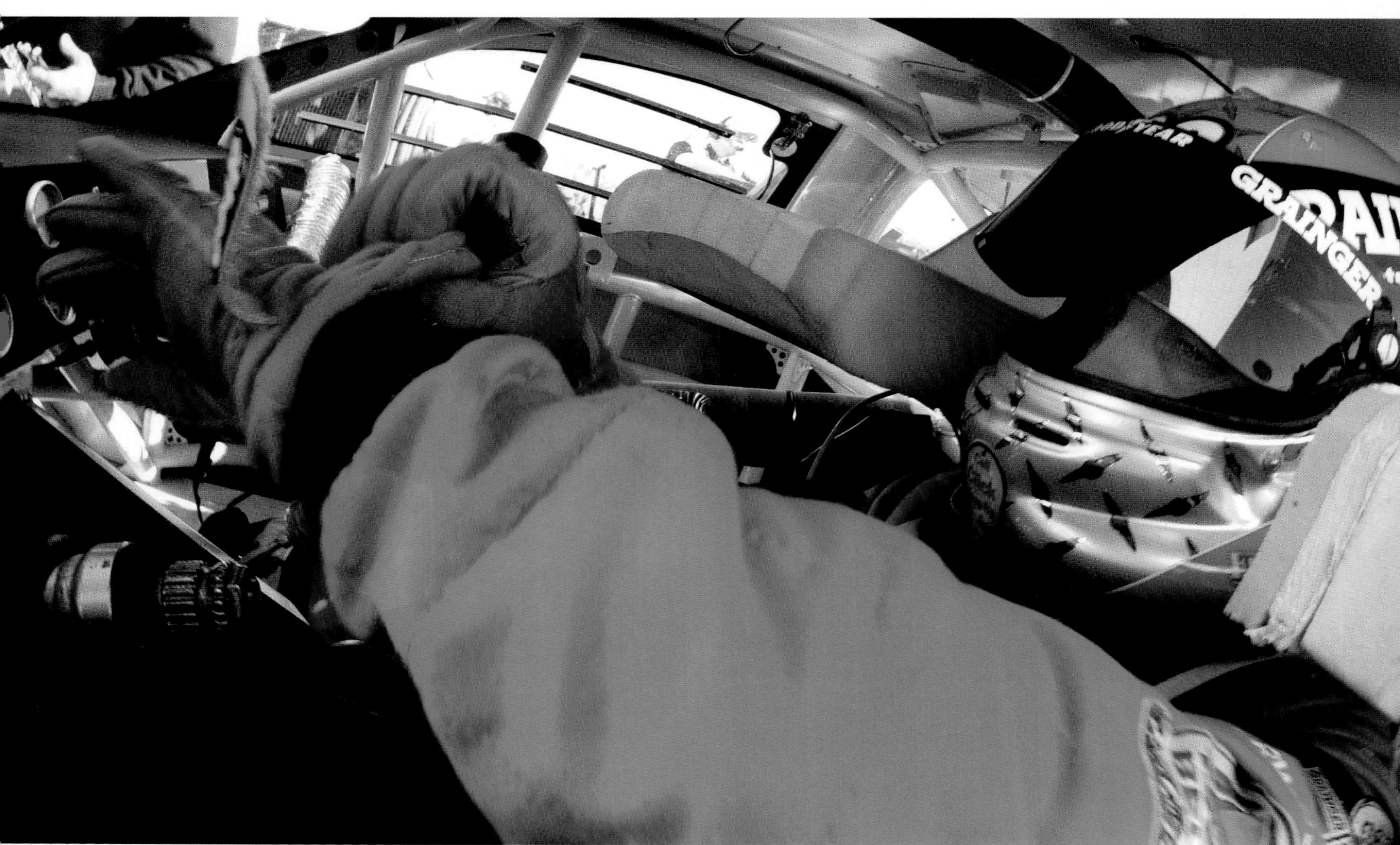

brett bodine

The 2002 season was another frustrating year for Bodine as he continued to struggle with his driver/owner role.

The limitations of trying function as NASCAR's only full-time owner and driver weighed heavily on Brett Bodine in 2002. The "middle" of the three racing Bodine bothers from Chemung, N.Y. (including older brother Geoff and younger brother Todd), Brett is a 17-year veteran of Winston Cup racing, but during that span, he has posted but one career victory.

That win came in the First Union 400 at now-defunct North Wilkesboro track in 1990, when Bodine was driving the No. 26 Quaker State car owned by Kenny Bernstein. Bodine also recorded his best-ever points finish that Season—12th.

Since he assumed the administrative and driving duties for his own team in 1996, however, Bodine has finished no better than 24th in points, and in 2002, after missing late-season races at both Dover and Kansas City, he slipped to the worst position of his career in the Winston Cup standings.

The season started more auspiciously than it ended. After qualifying 27th for the Daytona 500 in February, the 43-year-old Bodine came home 16th. His next strong showing came eight events later, when he managed a season-best finish of 13th at NASCAR's other restrictor-plate superspeedway, Talladega.

All told, Bodine led three laps in 2002—one each at Pocono, Sear's Point and New Hampshire, but the season wasn't what the last of NASCAR's privateers had hoped for. Mike Hillman started the season as Bodine's crew chief, but brother Geoff took over the pit crew in September. However, the change didn't bring the desired results as Bodine failed to make an impression in the remaining races. He eventually ended the season in a lowly 36th position in the final points standings.

Bodine has always been a capable driver, but he seldom has had the opportunity to drive the sort of equipment that can showcase his talent. Many owner/drivers—among them such luminaries as Ricky Rudd and Bill Elliott—have learned the hard way that it's more difficult to drive when you're worried about paying the bills.

ABOVE: The pressure of ownership has taken its toll on Brett Bodine's performances, and since 1996 he has struggled to find any consistency. He will be hoping the 2003 season is the start of a revival.

todd bodine

After a tumultous 2002 season that saw him sit out nine races, Bodine will be looking forward to a more secure future in 2003.

The 2002 campaign was to have been a season of plenty for journeyman driver Todd Bodine. After six seasons as NASCAR's "super sub," Bodine was to enjoy his first full-time Winston Cup ride since 1995, the last year he drove for Butch Mock. Considerable fanfare accompanied the announcement that Bodine would drive the No. 66 Kmart Ford for owner Travis Carter alongside teammate and long-time friend Joe Nemechek. Kmart's bankruptcy, however, ended that scenario before it began.

Without a sponsor for either team, Carter out of necessity parked Bodine's Ford after the third event of the season at Las Vegas, even though Bodine had won the pole for the race and led 17 laps. Nemechek competed in six events before Carter had to pull the plug on the No. 26 Ford. Nemechek went job-hunting and ultimately signed with Hendrick Motorsports for the 2003 season. Bodine missed nine races during Carter's sponsor search and returned to the No. 26 (formerly Nemechek's car number) for the June race at Pocono, qualified 39th and finished 18th, despite a blown motor on the next-to-last lap.

As the season progressed, Bodine put together a number of promising results, notably a seventh at Daytona, a sixth at New Hampshire, an eighth at Watkins Glen and a fifth at Richmond (after qualifying seventh). Bodine, however, has yet to shake his reputation for aggressiveness and impatience on the track. The driver once called a "cue-ball-headed fool" by Dale Earnhardt Jr., started a chain reaction collision that damage 10 cars when his tires left the asphalt at Charlotte and his car skidded through the grass. Bodine drew a fine and probation from NASCAR.

Regardless, Bodine is an extremely talented driver, as he proved long ago with Mock. But Bodine, who has driven at least one race for 14 different car owners, has seldom been in one ride long enough to prove himself. Barring the unexpected, 2003 could be the year.

ABOVE: Bodine posted several strong finishes in 2002 and the Haas/Carter team will expect more of the same from the No. 26 Ford in 2003.

Jamie McMurray

After winning in his second career Winston Cup start, McMurray heads into the 2003 season with high expectations.

Before the 2002 season began, you could have gotten the longest odds in the world against Jamie McMurray winning his first Winston Cup race before he won his first event in the Busch Series.

But circumstances conspired to elevate the 26-year-old driver from Joplin, Mo., to NASCAR's top series before he was scheduled to make the move. True, team owner Chip Ganassi had already decided to hire McMurray for the 2003 season—passing over several more experienced drivers—but when Sterling Marlin was sidelined with a cracked vertebra after the Kansas City race, McMurray earned a battlefield promotion to Winston Cup.

Almost immediately, he justified Ganassi's choice. In his second start, McMurray won the UAW-GM Quality 500 at Lowe's Motor Speedway in Charlotte on Oct.13. No other driver in the modern era of Winston Cup racing had won so quickly after entering the series. Two weeks later, in his third start, McMurray finished seventh in the NAPA 500 at Atlanta, and a week after that, he qualified second and finished 15th in the Pop Secret Microwave Popcorn 400 at Rockingham.

On Oct. 26, McMurray collected his first Busch Series win when he crossed the finish line at the end of the Aaron's 312 at Atlanta. One week later at Rockingham, he added a second Busch victory when Jeff Green and Michael Waltrip, who were running first and second at the time, wrecked on the final lap and allowed third-place McMurray to take the checkered flag.

In 2003, McMurray will run his first full Winston Cup schedule, though he won't have the benefit of Marlin's No. 40 Coors Light Dodge or Marlin's experienced pit crew. But based on his performance as a fill-in in 2002, McMurray has to be considered the leading candidate for rookie-of-the-year honors next season.

And who knows? Perhaps he'll duplicate the performances of Ryan Newman and Jimmie Johnson, who were serious contenders for the Winston Cup title during their rookie campaigns in 2002.

BELOW: McMurray's fairytale victory at Lowe's Motor Speedway was one of *the* stories of the 2002 Winston Cup Series. He will be a favorite for Rookie of the Year in 2003.

A.J. Foyt Racing

A legend on the track, A.J. Foyt is now looking to rekindle former glories as a team owner.

Team owner and legendary driver A.J. Foyt insisted his team will have a presence in Winston Cup racing in 2003. Foyt plans to promote his son, Larry Foyt, from NASCAR's Busch Series. Larry Foyt is scheduled to drive a Pontiac sponsored by the Harrah's casino chain, though the car number was still to be determined at season's end.

As of the final race of 2002 at Homestead-Miami Speedway, Foyt had not made a decision as to his choice to drive the No. 14 Conseco Pontiac in 2003. Foyt started the season with Stacy Compton behind the wheel, but released his driver after 19 races, with Compton a dismal 37th in points. Mike Wallace did a creditable job as Compton's replacement and made a strong case for his retention as full-time driver with an 11th place showing at Homestead.

At season's end, Wallace was considered the front-runner for the job, though Foyt had yet to make a final decision. The bottom line, though, was that Foyt was displeased with the effort of his Winston Cup operation and will enter the 2003 season determined to make a better showing. Foyt said he plans to spend more time at Winston Cup events in 2003, and that means the minions of the no-nonsense Texan had better toe the line.

TEAM STATISTICS

TEAM OWNER: A.J. FOYT

LARRY FOYT	
Driver Number:	**To Be Announced**
Crew Chief:	**To Be Announced**
Team Sponsor:	**Harrah's**

TO BE ANNOUNCED	
Driver Number:	**No. 14**
Crew Chief:	**To Be Announced**
Team Sponsor:	**Conseco**

Brett Bodine Racing

Brett Bodine heads into the 2003 season as the only remaining privateer competing in Winston Cup racing.

It's difficult enough trying to operate a single-car team. Great care must go into the choices of testing opportunities, and the chance to share track and set-up information from one driver to another simply isn't there. On top of that, try to operate your single-car team as an owner-driver. Since the retirement of long-time privateer Dave Marcis, Brett Bodine is the only full-time competitor in the Winston Cup Series who is trying to manage his entire operation and drive the car, too.

Bodine bought the No. 11 team from one of the most whimsicall characters in stock car racing, Junior Johnson. But with Bodine behind the wheel, the No. 11 hasn't approached the performance of its glory days under Johnson. A substantial part of the problem is financial—Bodine simply doesn't have the money to compete with the multi-car operations owned by such giants as Rick Hendrick, Jack Roush or Chip Ganassi on a week-to-week basis.

But Bodine perseveres. With engines supplied by Robert Yates Racing, the team performed creditably in the first two restrictor-plate races of 2002. And despite the lowest points finish of his career (he finished 36th in the final points standings), Bodine earned nearly $2 million in prize money—a nice pay day, but still far short of what it takes to operate a competitive Winston Cup team.

It's sad to say, but a driver of Bodine's ability will remain a long shot at best to win a Winston Cup race, as long as the team must function with second-tier equipment.

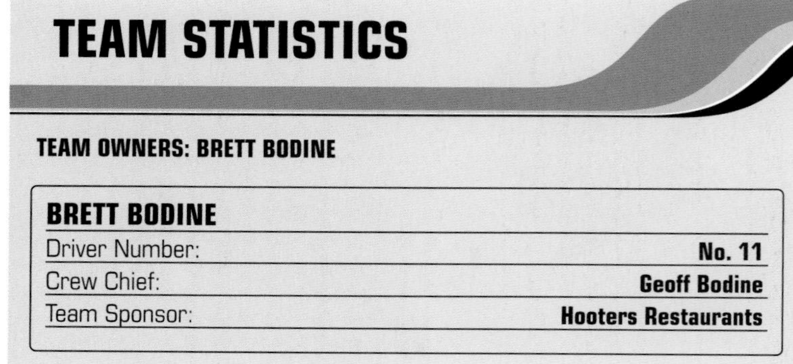
TEAM STATISTICS

TEAM OWNERS: BRETT BODINE

BRETT BODINE	
Driver Number:	**No. 11**
Crew Chief:	**Geoff Bodine**
Team Sponsor:	**Hooters Restaurants**

Haas-Carter Motorsports

Plagued by sponsorship problems in 2002, Travis Carter will be hoping for stability—and a victory—in 2003.

Crew chief Donnie Wingo has been a fixture at Haas/Carter Motorsports far longer than the driver of the No. 26 Ford, Todd Bodine. Wingo, however, is no stranger to the Bodine family—in 1989 he worked with Brett Bodine for 22 races, and in 1992 and 1993, Wingo collected three of his four victories as a Winston Cup crew chief with Geoff Bodine.

TEAM STATISTICS

TEAM OWNERS: TRAVIS CARTER

TODD BODINE	
Driver Number:	No. 26
Crew Chief:	Donnie Wingo
Team Sponsor:	Discover Card

Showing Todd Bodine the way to Victory Lane has proven somewhat more difficult. Kmart's demise late in 2001 cost owner Travis Carter the sponsor on which he had pinned his hopes for the season, and Bodine spent nine races on the sidelines until Discover Card came to the rescue. The bottom line is that Bodine hasn't won a Winston Cup race in more than a decade of trying (though he has been a prolific winner in the Busch Series), and Carter has never seen a car he owns beat the rest of the field to the checkered flag.

Both Carter and Bodine need (and deserve) a stable situation in which to bring their efforts to fruition. With Wingo, they have an experienced crew chief who has four Winston Cup wins to his credit. And don't forget, as a rookie crew chief in 1973, Carter guided Benny Parsons to the series championship. The added stability should help Bodine build on the few strong performances he posted in last year's Winston Cup as both team and driver search for consistency in 2003.

MB2 Motorsports

The 2003 season is one of change for MB2. Armed with a new driver and sponsor, they will be looking for a change in fortunes, too.

Jerry Nadeau did little to inspire confidence in his new owners for 2003. First of all, the Danbury, Conn., driver was released from Hendrick Motorsports' No. 25 Chevrolet before mid-season 2002 after a series of disappointing performances. Thereafter, Nadeau accepted a variety of assignments as a substitute driver. But after posting his best finish of the season (13th at Charlotte in the No. 44 Petty Enterprises car), since his eighth-place result in the No. 25 at Bristol in March, Nadeau broke his shoulder and cracked two ribs in a go-kart accident and was unavailable for the final five races of 2002.

The good news is that the driver Nadeau replaces in the No. 36 Pontiac has been mired in mediocrity for the past eight seasons. Ken Schrader hasn't won a race since 1991 and hasn't achieved a points finish better than 10th since 1994.

Owner Tom Beard felt it was time for a change and hired Nadeau for 2003. Nadeau, at least, has shown the capacity for running up front in recent years. He won at Atlanta in the fall 2000 and was leading the same race in 2001 when he ran out of fuel on the final lap.

The MB2 team loses its M&M's sponsorship to Robert Yates Racing and driver Elliott Sadler for the 2003 season. The U.S. Army will sponsor the No. 36 car for 27 races in 2003 and will serve as an associate sponsor for the other nine races. And the MB2 team made a major coup late in the season when it secured the services of crew chief Ryan Pemberton.

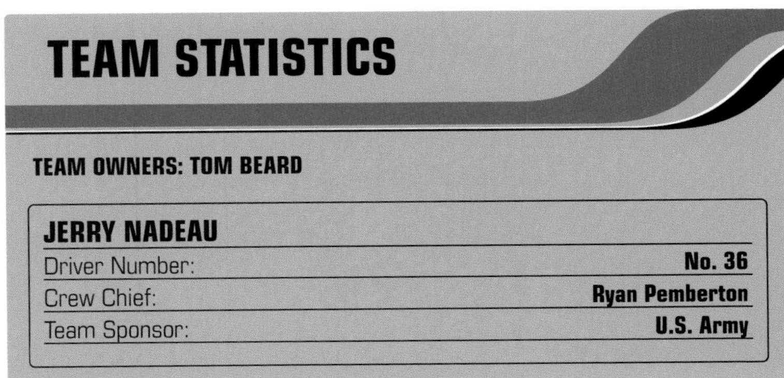

TEAM STATISTICS

TEAM OWNERS: TOM BEARD

JERRY NADEAU	
Driver Number:	No. 36
Crew Chief:	Ryan Pemberton
Team Sponsor:	U.S. Army

the tracks

The Winston Cup Series now visits some 24 different locations during a season. From the historic Daytona International Speedway to "The Desert Jewel" in Arizona, from the triangle at Pocono to the famed Watkins Glen road course, each track presents a unique challenge for both driver and team.

RIGHT: A bird's-eye view of Bristol Motor Speedway.

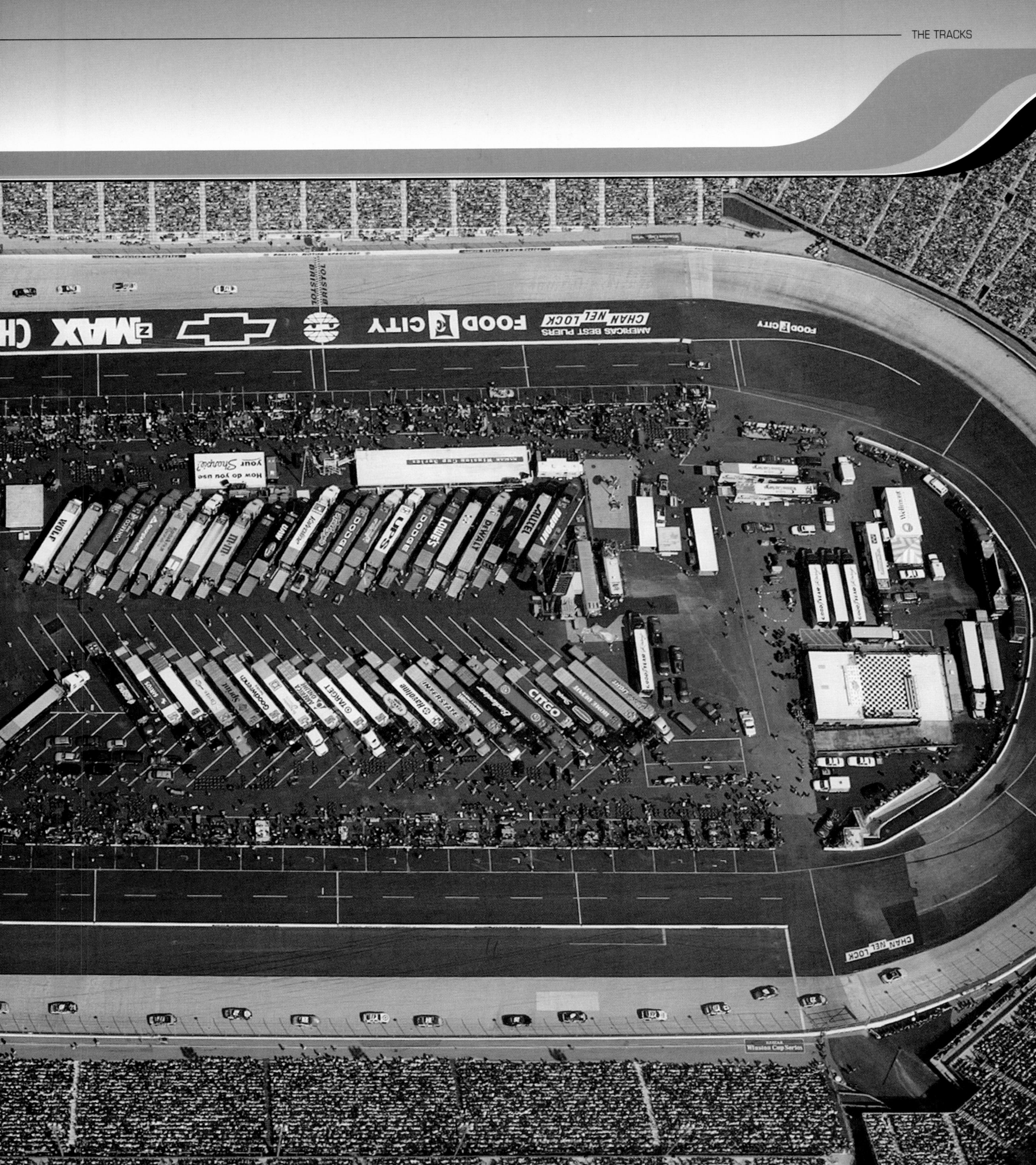
FOOD CITY
CHANNELLOCK
AMERICAS BEST PLIERS
BRISTOL
How do you use your Sharpie?
WOLF
DODGE
UPS
Lowe's
DEWALT
DUPONT
CITGO
TARGET
Havoline
INTERSTATE

Atlanta Motor Speedway

Reconfigured in 1997, with the start/finish line moved to the old backstretch, Atlanta is the fastest track on the Winston Cup circuit.

Opened in 1960 during the South's first major speedway building boom, Atlanta Motor Speedway is a 1.54-mile oval that has become Winston Cup racing's fastest track since the introduction of carburetor restrictor plates at Daytona and Talladega in 1988. Located south of Atlanta on Highways 19 and 41 in Hampton, Ga., the track is roughly equidistant between I-85 to the west and I-75 to the east. Atlanta hosts two Winston Cup races each year, the first in March and the second in late October to early November. Often in the past, the fall race has been crucial in determining the series championship.

The four turns at Atlanta Motor Speedway are banked at 24 degrees, with the straights banked at 5 degrees. Owned by O. Bruton Smith of Speedway Motorsports, Inc., the sister track to Lowe's Motor Speedway in Charlotte underwent a reconfiguration in 1997, when the start/finish line was moved from the traditional frontstretch to what had been the backstretch. Smith acquired ownership of the facility in 1990, and since then, elaborate renovations have rendered Atlanta one of the most modern multipurpose speedways on the NASCAR circuit.

In qualifying for the NAPA 500 in November of 1997, Jeff Bodine toured Atlanta Motor Speedway in an amazing 28.074 seconds for a record speed of 197.478 mph. Atlanta was a particular favorite of the late Dale Earnhardt, who recorded the next-to-last of his 76 Winston Cup victories there in the fall of 2000. All told, Earnhardt won nine races at Atlanta, a total unequaled by any other driver.

TRACK STATISTICS

An increase in facilities has improved this venue to the extent that it can now accommodate more than just speedway racing.

TRACK BIO	
Location:	**Hampton, GA**
Opened:	**1960**
Races hosted:	**Atlanta 500**
	Napa 500
Banking/Turns:	**24 degrees/4**
Distance:	**1.54 miles**
Shape:	**Oval**

RECORDS

Winston Cup Race Record:
D. Earnhardt 163.633mph
12 Nov. 1995

Winston Cup Qualifying Record:
G. Bodine 197.478mph
16 Nov. 1997

BELOW: Since 1988, when NASCAR introduced carburetor restrictor plates at Daytona and Talladega, Atlanta has been the fastest track on the circuit.

Bristol Motor Speedway

Anticipation for races at "Thunder Valley" is extremely high, as is the demand for tickets to one of NASCAR's most popular venues.

ABOVE: The half-mile known as "Thunder Valley" is one of NASCAR's most popular venues.

Another of Speedway Motorsports properties, Bristol is the second shortest track on the Winston Cup circuit at .533 miles—but it's second to none in excitement. For one thing, the track is banked 36 degrees in the corners and 16 degrees on the 650-foot straights, making "Thunder Valley" the fastest half-mile track in the world. Jeff Gordon set the qualifying record of 127.216 mph in March of 2002.

Built in 1961 just off Highway 394 near the Tennessee-Virginia border, the track was developed by Carl Moore, Larry Carrier and R.G. Pope. In the 32 years since Bristol Motor Speedway hosted its first NASCAR race in 1961, the seating capacity has grown from 18,000 to a phenomenal 147,000. Jack Smith won the inaugural Volunteer 500 with relief driving help from Johnny Allen, after legendary country music star Brenda Lee opened the show with the national anthem.

In 1992, Bristol was resurfaced with concrete, and in August of that year, the fabled oval became the first to host a Winston Cup event on an all-concrete track. The most popular short track on the circuit hosts two events per year—in the spring and fall—and tickets are always in strong demand. It's advisable to order early. Darrell Waltrip is the all-time Winston Cup winner at Thunder Valley; he collected 12 of his 84 victories at Bristol.

TRACK STATISTICS

Resurfaced in 1992 with concrete, the capacity of this venue has increased over 10-fold as attendance has grown.

TRACK BIO

Location:	**Bristol, TN**
Opened:	**1961**
Races hosted:	**Food City 500**
	Sharpie 500
Banking/Turns:	**36 degrees/4**
Distance:	**.533 mile**
Shape:	**Oval**

RECORDS

Winston Cup Race Record:
C. Glotzbach 101.074mph
11 July 1971

Winston Cup Qualifying Record:
J. Gordon 127.216mph
24 March 2002

California Speedway

The track that brought oval racing back to the Golden State is wide enough to allow NASCAR's top stars to race comfortably side by side.

Given that California Speedway was built by Roger Penske before its subsequent sale to International Speedway Corporation, it should come as no surprise that the superspeedway that opened in Fontana in 1997 bears a strong resemblance to its sister track in Michigan. In fact, both are 2.0-mile "D"-shaped ovals. The primary difference lies in the degree of banking in the corners. California is banked at 14 degrees in the four turns, compared to 18 degrees at Michigan. As a result, California is a slightly slower speedway, with a qualifying record of 187.432 mph set by Ryan Newman in April of 2002 (contrasted to Dale Earnhardt Jr.'s 191.149 at Michigan).

California Speedway is located at 9330 Cherry Avenue in Fontana, approximately 40 miles east of Los Angeles. The frontstretch, which includes the 11-degree-banked tri-oval, measures 3,100 feet, and the 3-degree-banked backstretch is 2,500 feet long. The length of the two straights puts a premium on horsepower, but the relatively flat corners also require a car to handle properly. Like Michigan, California is a speedway where fuel mileage can figure prominently in the outcome. Jeff Gordon won the inaugural race there in 1997.

TRACK STATISTICS

Now owned by the International Speedway Corporation, the events at this track continue a tradition of the sport at California ovals that dates back to April 1951.

TRACK BIO

Location:	**Fontana, CA**
Opened:	**1997**
Races hosted:	**Napa Auto Parts 500**
Banking/Turns:	**14 degrees/4**
Distance:	**2 miles**
Shape:	**Oval**

RECORDS

Winston Cup Race Record:
J. Gordon 155.012mph
22 June 1997

Winston Cup Qualifying Record:
R. Newman 187.432mph
26 April 2002

BELOW: The California Speedway plays host to the NAPA Auto Parts 500, a Winston Cup favorite.

Chicagoland Speedway

One of the most recent additions to the Winston Cup Series, Chicagoland produced but one winner in its first two seasons—Kevin Harvick.

ABOVE: Kevin Harvick won at Chicagoland as a rookie in 2001, then repeated the feat a year later.

A testament to the growing popularity of Winston Cup racing and its rapid expansion into the Midwest, Chicagoland Speedway opened to great fanfare in 2001. Accessible from downtown Chicago via interstate highway, Chicagoland is situated between Laraway Road and Schweitzer Road in Joliet. Race fans who want to avoid a lengthy car commute can take the Metra Rock Island District train line to Joliet Station, whence a bus will take them by restricted access highway to the speedway.

The track itself is a 1.5-mile tri-oval with 18-degree banking in the four turns. The tri-oval is banked at 11 degrees and the backstretch at 5 degrees. Chicagoland's most prominent feature is the 2,400-foot frontstretch that allows the Winston Cup cars to carry tremendous speed into the entrance to Turn 1. When Todd Bodine set the track qualifying record before the inaugural 400-mile Winston Cup event in 1993, he completed a lap in 29.393 seconds, at 183.717 mph.

Chicagoland is owned by Raceway Associates, LLC, a partnership that includes International Speedway Corporation and Indianapolis Motor Speedway president Tony George. In addition to a 400-mile Winston Cup race in July, the speedway hosts NASCAR's Busch Series as well as the IRL. Kevin Harvick won the first Cup race held at the new track on July 14, 2001.

TRACK STATISTICS

One of the newest venues for NASCAR, this track can accommodate up to 75,000 spectators at a race.

TRACK BIO

Location:	**Joliet, IL**
Opened:	**2001**
Races hosted:	**Tropicana 400**
Banking/Turns:	**18 degrees/4**
Distance:	**1.5 miles**
Shape:	**Tri-Oval**

RECORDS

Winston Cup Race Record:
K. Harvick 121.200mph
15 July 2001

Winston Cup Qualifying Record:
T. Bodine 183.717mph
13 July 2001

Darlington Raceway

NASCAR's first superspeedway, Darlington Raceway continues to host one of Winston Cup's most prestigious events—the Southern 500.

ABOVE: The "Lady in Black" is the oldest superspeedway built specifically for stock car racing.

Known as "The Lady in Black" or "The Track Too Tough to Tame," Darlington Raceway is the oldest superspeedway built specifically for NASCAR racing.

The egg-shaped oval has hosted the Southern 500, one of the three most prestigious races in the Winston Cup Series, since the track opened in 1950. Johnny Mantz notched his only victory in NASCAR's elite series in the inaugural event.

Located just off Highway 151 on the west side of Darlington, S.C., the speedway measures 1.366 miles, with 25-degree banking in Turns 1 and 2 and 23-degree banking in Turns 3 and 4. Because of the asymmetrical shape of the corners at each end of the track, crew chiefs must arrive at a workable compromise in the set-up when preparing the cars for their drivers. Inevitably, even the best-handling cars are likely to pick up a "Darlington stripe," the result of contact with the concrete retaining wall at the exit of what is now Turn 2.

Built by Harold Brasington and later acquired by International Speedway Corporation, Darlington Raceway holds a Winston Cup race in March in addition to the Southern 500, which is a Labor Day weekend tradition.

In 1997 a reconfiguration of the track moved the start/finish line from the frontstretch to the backstretch. Ward Burton holds the qualifying record at Darlington at 173.797 mph (28.295 seconds), set during time trials for the 1996 TranSouth 400. In 2002, Jeff Gordon tied Cale Yarborough for most Southern 500 victories with five.

TRACK STATISTICS

The first race to be held at this track saw 75 cars assemble to fight for a prize of $25,000 and qualifying took two weeks.

TRACK BIO

Location:	**Darlington, SC**
Opened:	**1950**
Races hosted:	**Carolina Dodge Dealers 400** **Mountain Dew Southern 500**
Banking/Turns:	**25/23 degrees/4**
Distance:	**1.366 miles**
Shape:	**Oval**

RECORDS

W/Cup 500 mile Race Record:
D. Earnhardt 139.958mph
28 March 1993

W/Cup 400 mile Race Record:
D. Pearson 132.703mph
11 May 1968

Winston Cup Qualifying Record:
W. Burton 173.797mph
22 March 1996

Daytona International Speedway

Speed Weeks at Daytona in February, culminating in the Daytona 500, may be the most exciting season-opening event in major league sports.

Opened in 1959, Daytona International Speedway is the home of NASCAR's most important race, the Daytona 500. The 2.5-mile superspeedway also serves a dual function as the headquarters of NASCAR. Located at 1801 West International Speedway Boulevard (Highway 92) approximately a half-mile east of I-95 in Daytona Beach, the tri-oval shaped track is banked 31 degrees in the four turns and 18 degrees on the tri-oval section. In addition to the Daytona 500, which takes place at the end of Speed Weeks each February, the Speedway also hosts the Pepsi 400 over the July 4 weekend. The February line-up also includes the Bud Shootout, a non-points race for pole winners from the previous season.

Because of the enormity of the speedway and the length of the straights (3,800 feet for the frontstretch, 3,400 for the backstretch), aerodynamics are critically important to racing at Daytona. Because "drafting" is such an essential element at NASCAR's largest tracks, cars at Daytona tend to run in a large pack at speeds approaching 200 mph. Nevertheless, set-up and handling through the corners are equally important to a driver hoping to win the 500, given that a perfectly prepared car can go full-throttle around the entire speedway.

Back in the 1980s, in fact, cars were circling Daytona International Speedway at speeds that were considered too fast to be safe, both for the drivers and the fans in the stands. After Bobby Allison's horrendous crash at Talladega in 1987, NASCAR began requiring carburetor restrictor plates, designed to reduce horsepower, on all cars racing at the circuit's two largest speedways. Consequently, Bill Elliott's 1987 Daytona qualifying record of 210.364 mph still stands.

TRACK STATISTICS

The Daytona 500 in 1979 was the first event that CBS TV committed to cover flag-to-flag, and ratings swelled as the race progressed to a close and dramatic finale.

TRACK BIO

Location:	**Daytona Beach, FL**
Opened:	**1959**
Races hosted:	**Budweiser Shootout Gatorade 125s Daytona 500 Pepsi 400**
Banking/Turns:	**31 degrees/4**
Distance:	**2.5 miles**
Shape:	**Tri-Oval**

RECORDS

W/Cup 500 mile Race Record:
B. Baker 177.602mph
17 Feb. 1980

W/Cup 400 mile Race Record:
B. Allison 173.473mph
4 July 1980

Winston Cup Qualifying Record:
B. Elliott 210.364mph
9 Feb. 1987

BELOW: Each February, Daytona International Speedway hosts stock car racing's premier event, the legendary Daytona 500. Last year's race was won by Ward Burton.

Dover Downs International Speedway

The concrete-surfaced Monster Mile contains a horse track within its perimeter, but it's the speedway that produces the real action.

Opened in 1969 and located at 1131 North Dupont Highway in Dover, Del., the "Monster Mile" is one of the most action-packed speedways on the Winston Cup circuit. The one-mile oval is banked 24 degrees in the four corners and 9 degrees on the straights, making Dover Downs one of the fastest tracks of its size in the country. Because the straights measure only 1,076 feet each, drivers spend the majority of each lap in the corners; as a consequence, spotters are especially important at Dover for their role in advising drivers about accidents that occur ahead of them on the track. Typically, a driver has only a split second to react to a wreck and escape trouble.

Richard Petty won the inaugural Winston Cup race at Dover, the Mason-Dixon 300 on July 6, 1969. The track hosted one event that year and a single Cup race in 1970. Since then, Dover has been the site of two Winston Cup races per year, held in June and September. Rusty Wallace set the track qualifying record of 159.946 mph (22.505 seconds) in September of 1999.

Before the 1995 season, Dover's asphalt surface was replaced with concrete, and before the fall race in 1997, the length of the Winston Cup events at the track was shortened from 500 miles to 400. (With average speeds that often failed to reach 120 mph, Dover races were some of the series' longest in duration.) Interestingly, the speedway derives its name "Dover Downs" from the horse track that encircles the infield.

TRACK STATISTICS

With a capacity of 140,000, Dover is one of the most popular destinations for sporting events in the northeast.

TRACK BIO	
Location:	**Dover, DE**
Opened:	**1969**
Races hosted:	**MBNA Platinum 400**
	MBNA All-American Heroes 400
Banking/Turns:	**24 degrees/4**
Distance:	**1 mile**
Shape:	**Oval**

RECORDS

Winston Cup Race Record:
M. Martin 132.719mph
21 Nov. 1997

Winston Cup Qualifying Record:
R. Wallace 159.964mph
25 Nov. 1999

BELOW: The Monster Mile, resurfaced with concrete in 1995, always produces action-packed racing.

Homestead-Miami Speedway

The track that has had several recent makeovers hosts the season-ending event—a race that might decide the series championship.

ABOVE: Tony Stewart won the first two Winston Cup races at Homestead-Miami Speedway.

Though Homestead-Miami Speedway opened in the fall of 1995, the 1.5-mile oval didn't host its first Winston Cup event until November of 1999—after the track had already undergone a major reconfiguration of its four corners.

Originally designed to resemble a "mini-Indianapolis" with flat, squared-off turns and short chutes at each end, the speedway now features a much different look as a continuous-turn oval.

Located near U.S. Highway 1 approximately 25 miles south of Miami International Airport, the track was developed by Ralph Sanchez and H. Wayne Huizenga. In 1997, Penske Motorsports and International Speedway Corporation came aboard as partners, and today ISC owns the facility. The racing complex boasts perhaps the most distinctive appearance on the Winston Cup circuit with its Art Deco architectural style.

After hosting NASCAR's Craftsman Truck Series and Busch Series during its first few years of operation, Homestead held its first Winston Cup event in November of 1999. Tony Stewart won the inaugural race and successfully defended his win the following year. Steve Park won the pole for the 2000 Pennzoil with a track-record run of 156.440 mph (34.518 seconds). In addition to NASCAR races, Homestead has proven an exciting venue for the world's top open-wheeled drivers.

TRACK STATISTICS

Since opening in 1995, this track has drawn something around 300,000 people on an annual basis to its events.

TRACK BIO

Location:	**Homestead, FL**
Opened:	**1995**
Races hosted:	**Ford 400**
Banking/Turns:	**6 degrees/4**
Distance:	**1.5 miles**
Shape:	**Oval**

RECORDS

Winston Cup Race Record:
T. Stewart 140.335mph
12 Nov. 1999

Winston Cup Qualifying Record:
S. Park 156.440mph
10 Nov. 2000

Indianapolis Motor Speedway

Racing's most storied venue, Indianapolis hosted one event per year, the Indianapolis 500, until stock cars invaded the Brickyard in 1994.

ABOVE: The famed Brickyard hosted its first Winston Cup race in 1994, and Jeff Gordon won it.

TRACK STATISTICS

Renowned for the Indy 500, which started in 1911, purists were in doubt as to the benefit of NASCAR coming to the track, but it has proved a spectacular success.

TRACK BIO	
Location:	**Indianapolis, IN**
Opened:	**1909**
Races hosted:	**Brickyard 400**
Banking/Turns:	**12 degrees/4**
Distance:	**2.5 miles**
Shape:	**Oval**

RECORDS

Winston Cup Race Record:
B. Labonte 155.912mph
5 Aug. 2000

Winston Cup Qualifying Record:
B. Bodine 181.072mph
4 Aug. 2000

America's most revered racing facility opened in August of 1909, nearly 40 years before the formation of NASCAR. The annual home of the Indianapolis 500, the vaunted Brickyard did not allow stock cars to compete on its hallowed asphalt until Aug. 6, 1994, when Jeff Gordon took the checkered flag at the end of the inaugural Brickyard 400. In less than a decade, however, the only Winston Cup race held annually at Indianapolis has become one of the most prestigious on the circuit.

Negotiating the four relatively flat corners, banked at 9 degrees 12 minutes, can be problematic, even though the Winston Cup cars travel nearly 50 mph slower per lap than do the open-wheeled Indy Cars. Handling is a major issue at the Brickyard, where maintaining momentum off the second and fourth turns is crucial to success. It should come as no surprise that the winners of the first nine Brickyard 400s are some of NASCAR's most talented drivers: Gordon (three times), Dale Jarrett (twice), Dale Earnhardt, Ricky Rudd, Bobby Labonte and Bill Elliott.

With more than 250,000 permanent seats, Indianapolis Motor Speedway, located at 4790 West 16th Street approximately three miles east of the I-465 loop, is the world's largest sporting facility. In addition to the Indy 500 and Brickyard 400, the speedway also plays host to the United States Grand Prix for Formula One cars, which debuted at the venerable track in 2000. Tony Stewart holds the qualifying record for Winston Cup cars at 182.960 mph (49.704 seconds), the pole-winning speed for the 2002 race.

Kansas Speedway

Chassis set-up is critically important at Kansas Speedway because of the relatively shallow banking in the corners of the 1.5-mile tri-oval.

A newcomer to Winston Cup racing in 2001, Kansas Speedway opened for business on July 6, 2001 as a new addition to the International Speedway Corporation's portfolio of racing facilities. The first Winston Cup race at Kansas didn't take place until Sept. 30 that year, with Jeff Gordon adding to his impressive list of victories in inaugural races.

Kansas Speedway, like many of the other modern tracks on the circuit, is a 1.5-mile tri-oval. What sets this speedway apart, however, is the relatively shallow banking in the turns (15 degrees), as compared to the steeper Charlotte, Atlanta or Texas. Kansas is banked 10.4 degrees on the frontstretch and 5 degrees on the backstretch. In addition to its annual fall Winston Cup race, Kansas also hosts the Busch Series, Craftsman Truck Series and Indy Racing League.

Jason Leffler won the pole for the 2001 Protection 400 at 176.499 mph (30.595 seconds), setting a de facto track record in the process. Kansas Speedway, located near the intersection of I-70 and I-435 approximately 15 miles west of downtown Kansas City, Kan., provides grandstand seating for 78,000 fans, and those who wish to attend the Cup event there are advised to order early. The track's 32 luxury boxes sold out two years before the first Winston Cup event took place. Baseball Hall of Fame inductee George Brett purchased the first Fan P.A.S.S. (Preferred Access Speedway Seating).

TRACK STATISTICS

Built to answer the demand for more racing in the midwest, Kansas has done so in style with its fantastic facilities.

TRACK BIO

Location:	**Kansas City, KS**
Opened:	**2001**
Races hosted:	**Protection One 400**
Banking/Turns:	**15 degrees/4**
Distance:	**1.5 miles**
Shape:	**Tri-Oval**

RECORDS

Winston Cup Race Record:
J. Gordon 110.576mph
30 Sept. 2001

Winston Cup Qualifying Record:
J. Leffler 176.449mph
28 Sept. 2001

BELOW: Jeff Gordon won the inaugural race at Kansas in 2000 and returned to Victory Lane in 2001.

Las Vegas Motor Speedway

The jewel in the desert provides exciting side-by-side racing.

A relatively flat 1.5-mile oval with a sweeping 2,275-foot frontstretch, Las Vegas Motor Speedway is a jewel in the desert surrounding the glitz capital of the world. Located at 7000 Las Vegas Boulevard North approximately 10 miles northeast of the Vegas strip, the track is banked modestly at 12 degrees in the four corners and 9 degrees on the frontstretch.

Owned and operated by Speedway Motorsports, Inc., Las Vegas Motor Speedway opened in 1996 and held its first Winston Cup race on March 1, 1998. Mark Martin won the inaugural Las Vegas 400, and in fact, Jack Roush-owned Fords captured the first three Cup races held there, with Jeff Burton winning in 1999 and 2000. Jeff Gordon broke the string with a victory in the No. 24 Chevy in 2001, and Sterling Marlin added the Dodge name to the winner's list in 2002.

With grandstand seating for 126,000, Las Vegas can accommodate a large confluence of race fans. It's advisable to leave early for the track on race days, since the two main arteries to the track, I-15 and Las Vegas Boulevard, tend to become jammed as the start time nears. Todd Bodine holds the qualifying record at Las Vegas—he completed a lap at an average speed of 172.849 mph in March of 2002. In addition to the main speedway, Vegas also features a 2.5-mile road course and a 4,000-foot dragway.

TRACK STATISTICS

When it was built, this track was the first to appear in the southwest for 20 years. It now provides something for every age in terms of motorsport.

TRACK BIO

Location:	**Las Vegas, NV**
Opened:	**1996**
Races hosted:	**UAW-Daimler Chrysler 400**
Banking/Turns:	**12 degrees/4**
Distance:	**1.5 miles**
Shape:	**Tri-Oval**

RECORDS

Winston Cup Race Record:
M. Martin 146.530mph
1 March 1998

Winston Cup Qualifying Record:
R. Rudd 172.563mph
3 March 2000

BELOW: Located in the desert on the outskirts of Las Vegas, the 1.5-mile track can accommodate more than 130,000 fans.

Lowe's Motor Speedway

With the majority of NASCAR teams located within a short drive from Charlotte, Lowe's serves as a "home track" for many of the stars.

Formerly Charlotte Motors Speedway until Lowe's paid handsomely for the naming rights, this 1.5-mile quad-oval is the showpiece of the Speedway Motorsports portfolio. Located just off Highway 29 in Harrisburg, N.C., Lowe's Motor Speedway is the annual site of NASCAR's longest race, the Coca-Cola 600 (formerly World 600) on Memorial Day weekend.

With turns banked at 24 degrees and the straights banked at 5 degrees, Lowe's is one of the faster "intermediate" superspeedways, as Jimmie Johnson's qualifying record of 186.464 mph will attest. Built in 1959 by Speedway Motorsports chairman O. Bruton Smith and his business partner of the time, stock car driver Curtis Turner, Lowe's opened in June of 1960 with the inaugural World 600.

The speedway hosts a 500-mile race in the fall. In addition, Lowe's has been home to 17 of the 18 runnings of The Winston all-star race, a non-points event that traditionally takes place eight days before the Coca-Cola 600. Darrell Waltrip and Bobby Allison are tied for most wins at Lowe's with six each. With five victories in the 600, Waltrip is the only driver to win NASCAR's longest race more than three times.

Lowe's Motor Speedway's management, headed by Smith and track president H.A. "Humpy" Wheeler, has always been innovative. In 1992 the Lowe's was the first superspeedway to install a lighting system that allowed night racing. Lowe's was also the first track to build condominiums with a view of the speedway. Residents can watch the action from their perches above Turn 1.

BELOW: Lowe's Motor Speedway is the site of the world's longest stock car race, the Coca-Cola 600.

TRACK STATISTICS

A crowd of 35,000 saw the first race at this venue, but the capacity has now grown to an awesome 100,000.

TRACK BIO	
Location:	**Concord, NC**
Opened:	**1959**
Races hosted:	**The Winston** **Coca-Cola 600** **UAW-GM Quality 500**
Banking/Turns:	**24 degrees/4**
Distance:	**1.5 miles**
Shape:	**Quad-Oval**

RECORDS

W/Cup 600 mile Race Record:
B. Labonte 151.952mph
28 May 1995

W/Cup 500 mile Race Record:
J. Gordon 160.306mph
11 Oct. 1999

Winston Cup Qualifying Record:
J. Johnson 186.464mph
24 May 2002

Martinsville Speedway

A traditional short track in southern Virginia, Martinsville provides race fans with plenty of bump-and-bang excitement.

ABOVE: The paper clip–shaped speedway is one of the few traditional short tracks left on the Winston Cup circuit.

A narrow .526-mile oval designed in the shape of a paper clip, Martinsville Speedway is a demanding short track that invariably takes its toll on equipment. Unwary drivers can wear out their brakes in a hurry as they enter the 12-degree-banked turns from straights that are absolutely flat. Because the straights are a mere 800 feet long, handling and the ability to accelerate off the corners without spinning the tires are of paramount importance here.

Opened in 1947, and owned and operated by W. Clay Campbell, Martinsville Speeedway held its first race in NASCAR's foremost series in May of 1956, when Buck Baker took the checkered flag in the Virginia 500 en route to the first of his two Winston Cup championships. Located on the south side of town near Highway 220, the speedway can provide grandstand seating for 91,000 fans.

Tony Stewart set the qualifying record of 95.371 mph in September of 2000, when he won the pole for the NAPA 500. Throughout the years, however, no driver was as dominant at Martinsville as Richard Petty, who picked up 15 of his record 200 victories at the half-mile track. Another short track expert, Darrell Waltrip, won 15 times at Martinsville, which annually hosts a pair of Winston Cup races—in April and October. Rusty Wallace leads active drivers with six Martinsville wins, tied for third all-time with Cale Yarborough and the late Dale Earnhardt.

TRACK STATISTICS

Everyone acknowledges that Martinsville has developed into one of the most attractive and well-equipped venues on the NASCAR circuit.

TRACK BIO

Location:	**Martinsville, VA**
Opened:	**1947**
Races hosted:	**Virginia 500**
	Martinsville 500
Banking/Turns:	**12 degrees/4**
Distance:	**.526 mile**
Shape:	**Oval**

RECORDS

Winston Cup Race Record:
J. Gordon 82.223mph
22 Aug. 1996

Winston Cup Qualifying Record:
T. Stewart 95.371mph
29 Sept. 2000

Michigan International Speedway

A huge facillity with a sweeping frontstretch, Michigan can lull a driver into a false sense of security—before disaster strikes.

A wide "D"-shaped oval that measures two miles around, Michigan International Speedway is the place to go for side-by-side high-speed racing. Situated on a 1,200-acre tract of land in the Irish Hills of southeastern Michigan—near the intersection of Highways 12 and 50 south of Jackson, about 75 miles southwest of downtown Detroit—MIS features 18-degree banking in the four turns and 12-degree banking on the frontstretch.

The banking and the wide racing groove (or variety of grooves) allow for three-wide and occasionally four-wide racing. Current qualifying speeds at Michigan, which is not a restrictor-plate track, are comparable to those at Daytona and Talladega, where carburetors are restricted to reduce horsepower. Dale Earnhardt Jr. holds the MIS qualifying record at 191.149 mph, his polewinning speed for Pepsi 400 in August of 2000.

Now owned by International Speedway Corporation—after its tenure in the hands of Penske Motorsports—Michigan hosts two 400-mile Winston Cup events each year, in June and August. David Pearson heads the all-time victory list at Michigan with nine. Bill Elliott leads active drivers with seven wins. Designed by Charles Moneypenny, who also designed Daytona International Speedway, Michigan opened in 1968. Cale Yarborough recorded the first of his eight victories at Michigan in the inaugural Winston Cup race, the Motor State 500 on June 15, 1969.

The original layout at MIS included an interior and exterior road course designed by Formula One star Stirling Moss. Neither course has seen competition since 1984, but law enforcement agencies occasionally use them for passenger car testing.

TRACK STATISTICS

Drafting, speed and competition have made the Michigan track among the most popular stops on the tour.

TRACK BIO

Location:	**Brooklyn, MI**
Opened:	**1968**
Races hosted:	**Sirius Satellite Radio 400**
Banking/Turns:	**18 degrees/4**
Distance:	**2 miles**
Shape:	**Tri-Oval**

RECORDS

Winston Cup Race Record:
D. Jarrett 173.997mph
13 June 1999

Winston Cup Qualifying Record:
D. Earnhardt Jr. 191.149mph
18 Aug. 2000

BELOW: The high-speed two-mile oval at Michigan lends itself to side-by-side racing.

New Hampshire International Speedway

Race weekends attract race fans from New England and beyond. When NASCAR visits, the peaceful town of Loudon is bustling with activity.

ABOVE: NASCAR's northernmost venue hosts Winston Cup events in July and September.

TRACK STATISTICS

Accommodating as it does some 101,000 spectators, it is no wonder that New Hampshire International Speedway plays host to the largest sporting events in New England.

TRACK BIO	
Location:	**Loudon, NH**
Opened:	**1990**
Races hosted:	**New England 300**
	New Hampshire 300
Banking/Turns:	**12 degrees/4**
Distance:	**1.058 miles**
Shape:	**Oval**

RECORDS

Winston Cup Race Record:
J. Burton 117.134mph
13 July 1997

Winston Cup Qualifying Record:
R. Wallace 132.089mph
7 July 2000

A bucolic location in New Hampshire hardly seems an ideal place to showcase a sport indigenous to the Southeast, but New Hampshire International Speedway has thrived as the host of two Winston Cup events per year—the first in July, the second in September. Nestled into the countryside next to Highway 106 between Loudon and Belmont, New Hampshire is a flat 1.058-mile oval that is banked 12 degrees in the turns and 2 degrees on the straights.

Owned by Bob Bahre and opened in 1990, New Hampshire held its first Winston Cup race in 1993. Rusty Wallace won the initial Slick 50 300 over Mark Martin and the late Davey Allison. Seven years later, Wallace set the track qualifying record of 132.089 mph during time trials for the thatlook.com 300 in July of 2000. Jeff Burton is the leading winner at NHIS with four victories. Jeff Gordon, with three wins, is the only other Winston Cup driver with more than one.

With grandstand seating for 91,000, New Hampshire routinely draws more than 100,000 fans for a Winston Cup event—there is no sporting event in New England that boasts a bigger crowd. In barely more than a decade since its opening in 1990, the motorsports complex at New Hampshire has proven itself a viable venue for a wide variety of speed sports, including Winston Cup, the Busch Series, the Craftsman Truck Series, the Busch North Series, the Featherlite Modified Series, CART, the Indy Racing League, Formula Ford 2000, Toyota Atlantic and Indy Lights.

North Carolina Speedway

A track that's difficult to master, "The Rock" has hosted the Winston Cup Series ever since the facility in Rockingham opened in 1965.

Known as "The Rock" for its proximity to Rockingham, N.C., North Carolina Speedway was the product of a joint venture between Darlington Speedway builder Harold Brasington and Bill Land, who owned the property along U.S. Highway 1 where NCS was constructed. Originally designed as a one-mile flat track, North Carolina Speedway held its first Winston Cup race, the American 500, in 1965, the year the track opened. In 1969, NCS was renovated to its present configuration of 1.017 miles, with 22-degree banking in Turns 1 and 2 and 25-degree banking in Turns 3 and 4.

Located just off Route 1, 10 miles north of Rockingham and 20 miles south of Pinehurst/Southern Pines, The Rock is easily accessible from the Piedmont, Sandhills and coastal areas of North and South Carolina. It sits across the street from another North Carolina Motorsports institution—Rockingham Dragway. Over the years, drivers have characterized the racing surface as one of the more abrasive on the circuit; consequently, tire wear is often of paramount concern at The Rock.

Each year, NCS host two Winston Cup events, the first typically a week after the Daytona 500, and the second during the closing weeks of the season in October or November. North Carolina Speedway has often figured prominently in the outcome of the Winston Cup points race. Rusty Wallace holds the qualifying record at The Rock, thanks to a 158.035 mph lap during time trials for the Dura-Lube/Kmart 400 in February of 2000. Richard Petty won 11 races at NCS to lead all drivers past or present.

TRACK STATISTICS

The current shape of this track was the result of its control being taken over by a local businessman, L. G. De Witt.

TRACK BIO	
Location:	**Rockingham, NC**
Opened:	**1969**
Races hosted:	**Subway 400** **Pop Secret Microwave Popcorn 400**
Banking/Turns:	**22/25 degrees/4**
Distance:	**1.017 miles**
Shape:	**Oval**

RECORDS

Winston Cup Race Record:
J. Burton 131.103mph
24 Oct. 1999

Winston Cup Qualifying Record:
R. Wallace 158.035mph
25 Feb. 2000

BELOW: Known as "The Rock," North Carolina Motorspeedway always provides race fans with plenty to cheer about.

Phoenix International Raceway

A track built on land that once belonged to the rattlesnakes, Phoenix features a configuration that tests the skills of the world's best.

ABOVE: A "flat" track in the Arizona desert, Phoenix presents a different challenge in every corner.

Situated at the base of the Estrella Mountains west of Phoenix, Ariz., Phoenix International Raceway presents a unique set of challenges for Winston Cup drivers. Conceived as a venue for open-wheeled racing, PIR opened in 1964, but it wasn't until 1988 that NASCAR first brought the Winston Cup Series to the one-mile flat track known as "The Desert Jewel."

Though the Indy Cars have competed at PIR on 58 occasions, the track's NASCAR weekend in November is one of the most important sports events in Arizona. Not only do the Winston Cup cars race on the one-mile oval that presents a different set of challenges in every corner, but the weekend also includes the Busch Series, Craftsman Truck Series and Featherlite Southwest Series. Located at 7602 South 115th Ave. approximately 20 miles west-southwest of the downtown area, PIR is readily accessible from I-10.

PIR is one of the circuit's trickiest flat tracks, with an imposing concrete wall looming at the exit of Turn 2. The first two turns are banked at a modest 11 degrees, with Turns 3 and 4 banked at 9 degrees. The straights are flat. The late Alan Kulwicki won the first Winston Cup race held at PIR, the Checker 500, in 1988. Rusty Wallace set the track record of 134.178 mph during qualifying for the 2000 Checker/Dura-Lube 500. Jeff Burton (2000, 2001) and the late Davey Allison (1991, 1992) are the only back-to-back winners at Phoenix.

TRACK STATISTICS

With continuing development since its opening in 1964, this venue is now considered one of the country's best.

TRACK BIO

Location:	**Phoenix, AZ**
Opened:	**1964**
Races hosted:	**Checker Auto Parts 500**
Banking/Turns:	**11/9 degrees/4**
Distance:	**1 mile**
Shape:	**Oval**

RECORDS

Winston Cup Race Record:
T. Stewart 118.132mph
7 Nov. 1999

Winston Cup Qualifying Record:
R. Wallace 134.718mph
3 Nov. 2000

Pocono Raceway

Three-cornered Pocono often resembles the Bermuda Triangle, rather than a speedway in the Pennsylvania countryside.

Triangular-shaped Pocono Raceway is perhaps the most distinctive on the Winston Cup circuit. The 2.5-mile superspeedway features three unique corners —which don't resemble each other in the slightest. Accordingly, setting up a stock car to negotiate Pocono is a series of trade-offs and compromises. A car that will roll smoothly through 14-degree-banked Turn 1 might have trouble in Turn 2 (the Tunnel Turn), which flattens out to 8 degrees. The most critical corner, though, is No. 3, a tight turn banked at 6 degrees. It is absolutely imperative that the car carry momentum into the 3,740-foot frontstretch, but then again, a car that's set up for an ideal exit from Turn 3 won't be perfect in Turn 1.

Over the years, Winston Cup drivers have learned to incorporate road racing skills into their repertoires at Pocono. It is now commonplace to shift gears during a trip around the 2.5-mile track, which opened in 1968 on Long Pond Road, just off of Highway 115, south of I-80. Richard Petty won the first Winston Cup race held at the track, the 1974 Purolator 500. Tony Stewart holds the qualifying record of 172.391 mph, set during time trials for the 2000 Pocono 500. Bill Elliott has won five times at Pocono, which annually hosts Cup races in June and July. Wallace, Darrell Waltrip and the late Tim Richmond are tied for second with four wins each.

TRACK STATISTICS

It was once said that this track was built by committee, with its three-turn triangle, each with a different radius and angle.

TRACK BIO	
Location:	**Pocono, PA**
Opened:	**1968**
Races hosted:	**Pocono 500** **Pennsylvania 500**
Banking/Turns:	**14/8/6 degrees/3**
Distance:	**2.5 miles**
Shape:	**Tri-Oval**

RECORDS

Winston Cup Race Record:
R. Wallace 144.892mph
21 July 1996

Winston Cup Qualifying Record:
T. Stewart 172.391mph
21 July 2000

BELOW: The triangular configuration of this 2.5-mile superspeedway poses challenges to the crew chiefs trying to set up their cars.

Richmond International Raceway

At Richmond, race fans can't wait for the sun to go down. That's when the action starts at one of NASCAR's most popular short tracks.

A race under the lights at Richmond International Raceway is an experience unlike any other in NASCAR competition. The track that has undergone an abundance of changes since it opened in 1946 now produces some of the most spellbinding spectacles in stock car racing. RIR debuted as a half-mile dirt track, and Ted Horn won the first race held there in 1946. Though NASCAR's foremost series wouldn't visit Richmond until 1953, Red Byron won the first NASCAR sanctioned race staged in Virginia at RIR on May 16, 1948. Lee Petty triumphed in the first Winston Cup event there, the Richmond 200, on April 19, 1953.

As it is presently configured, Richmond's .75-mile oval was reconstructed in 1988 on the site of the old dirt track, which had been paved in 1968. The four turns are banked at 14 degrees. The frontstretch is banked at 8 degrees, and the backstretch flattens out to 2 degrees exiting the second corner. RIR is located in Henrico County, just outside the Richmond city limits near the junction of I-95 and I-64.

In May of 2002, Ward Burton bettered Jeff Gordon's 1999 qualifying record of 126.499 with a lap at 127.388 during time trials for the Pontiac Excitement 400. Richard Petty is the runaway career winner at RIR with 13 victories to his credit. Bob Allison is a distant second with seven wins, and Rusty Wallace leads active drivers with six.

TRACK STATISTICS

Recently refurbished, Richmond International Raceway is now one of the most modern tracks on the circuit.

TRACK BIO

Location:	**Richmond, VA**
Opened:	**1946**
Races hosted:	**Pontiac Excitement 400** **Chevy Monte Carlo 400**
Banking/Turns:	**14 degrees/4**
Distance:	**.75 mile**
Shape:	**Oval**

RECORDS

Winston Cup Race Record:
D. Jarrett 108.707mph
6 Sept. 1997

Winston Cup Qualifying Record:
W. Burton 127.388mph
13 May 2002

BELOW: A three-quarter-mile speedway that has undergone several reconstructions and reconfigurations, Richmond hosts two night races each year.

Sears Point (Infineon Raceway)

At Infineon Raceway, one of two road courses on the Winston Cup circuit, drivers get the chance to turn right as well as left for a change.

Located in the heart of California wine country at the intersection of Highways 37 and 121 in Sonoma, about 30 minutes north of San Francisco's famed Golden Gate Bridge, Infineon Raceway (formerly Sears Point Raceway before the influx of corporate dollars) offers Winston Cup drivers their first opportunity of the year to turn right. The 2.0-mile circuit, which features changes in elevation that are foreign to oval racing, is one of two road courses that host annual Winston Cup events.

NASCAR's elite division comes to Sonoma in June, but the Winston Cup stars have plied their trade at Infineon Raceway only since 1989, when Ricky Rudd won the Banquet 300 in a Buick. Road races in California, however, have long been a NASCAR tradition, dating to the early days at now-defunct Riverside. Infineon Raceway, in fact, existed long before a Winston Cup race ever took place there. Robert Marshall Jr. and Jim Coleman built the track as a 2.52-mile course on a 720-acre tract of land in 1968. Infineon has survived numerous changes in ownership and management over the years and now is owned and operated by Speedway Motorsports, Inc.

For Winston Cup racing, the course itself features 10 turns, the most exciting of which is the hairpin that represents a driver's last realistic chance to pass before the start/finish line. Jeff Gordon has won three races at Infineon, more than any other driver. Gordon also holds the track record of 93.699 mph, a mark he established during qualifying for the 2001 Dodge/Save Mart 350.

TRACK STATISTICS

There are few road courses on the NASCAR circuit and its location makes Infineon one of the most attractive.

TRACK BIO	
Location:	**Sonoma, CA**
Opened:	**1968**
Races hosted:	**Dodge/Save Mart 350**
Banking/Turns:	**n/a/10**
Distance:	**2 miles**
Shape:	**Road Course**

RECORDS

Winston Cup Race Record:
E. Irvan 81.412mph
7 June 1992

Winston Cup Qualifying Record:
J. Gordon 93.699mph
23 June 2001

ABOVE: The first of the road courses on the Winston Cup schedule, Infineon Raceway features 10 unique turns to test the drivers.

Talladega Superspeedway

The close, high-speed racing at Talladega will take your breath away. So will the violent, multi-car collisions that are all but inevitable.

The longest racetrack on the Winston Cup circuit, Talladega Superspeedway measures 2.66 miles, and drivers can hold the throttle wide open all the way around the colossal speedway. Like its sister track in Daytona, Talladega is a restrictor-plate venue. Though the cars don't travel as fast with their horsepower reduced, the use of restrictor plates tends to bunch the entire field in a large pack. Hence, drivers approach races at Talladega with a mixture of excitement and dread. Side-by-side racing is exhilarating at nearly 200 miles per hour, but one slip or bobble can send 20 cars spinning out of control, smashing into the retaining wall and into each other. That's what's known at Talladega as "The Big One."

The track is banked in the corners at 33 degrees and at 18 degrees in the tri-oval. Banking that steep ensures maximum speed around the circuit. Talladega Superspeedway opened in September of 1969 for the running of the first Talladega 500, a race that gave Richard Brickhouse his only career Winston Cup victory. In fact, the quirky nature of drafting at the Alabama track has helped a handful of relatively obscure drivers find Victory Lane. Dick Brooks, Lennie Pond, Ron Bouchard, Bobby Hillin Jr. and Phil Parsons each won once in NASCAR's elite series—and each picked up his lone victory at Talladega.

Located south of I-20 just off Highway 399 in Talladega, Ala., the speedway currently hosts two Winston Cup events per year, in April and October. Bill Elliot holds the qualifying record of 212.809 mph, set during time trials for the Winston 500 in 1987, the last year of unrestricted carburetors at Talladega and Daytona.

TRACK STATISTICS

Originally known as the Alabama International Motor Speedway, this track is one of the biggest and fastest in the country.

TRACK BIO	
Location:	**Talladega, AL**
Opened:	**1969**
Races hosted:	**Aaron's 499** **EA Sports 500**
Banking/Turns:	**33 degrees/4**
Distance:	**2.66 miles**
Shape:	**Tri-Oval**

RECORDS
Winston Cup Race Record:
M. Martin 188.354mph
10 May 1997
Winston Cup Qualifying Record:
B. Elliott 212.809mph
30 April 1987

ABOVE: At 2.66 miles, Talladega is the longest superspeedway on the Winston Cup circuit.

Texas Motor Speedway

Located in the heart of "Cow Country," Texas Motorspeedway brought Winston Cup racing back to the Lone Star state in 1997.

Very similar in configuration to Lowe's Motor Speedway in Charlotte, one of its sister tracks, Texas Motor Speedway is a 1.5-mile quad-oval that features 24-degree banking in the four turns and 5-degree banking on the straights. Located at 3601 Highway 144, west of I-35W in Fort Worth, TMS opened in 1996 under the banner of Speedway Motorsports, Inc. In the intervening six years Texas has overcome early problems with water seepage through the asphalt surface and lack of a second racing groove to become one of the Winston Cup Series, most exciting tracks. TMS has hosted an April Cup each year since 1997, when Jeff Burton won the inaugural Interstate Batteries 500.

Texas Motor Speedway has sent a different winner to Victory Lane for each of the six Winston Cup events held to date. Roush drivers Jeff Burton and Mark Martin won the first two races in Fords. Terry Labonte in 1999 and Dale Earnhardt Jr. in 2000 evened the score for Chevrolet with a pair of victories. It was Ford again in 2001, when Dale Jarrett beat Steve Park to the checkered flag. In 2002, Matt Kenseth became the third different driver from the Roush stable to win in Cow Town. In capturing the pole for the 2002 Samsung/Radio Shack 500, Bill Elliott smashed Terry Labonte's previous qualifying record by more than two miles per hour in posting an average speed of 194.224.

TRACK STATISTICS

Uniquely, the first Winston Cup race on this circuit had no pole winner but gave the 30 places in the field to the top 30 cars in the points standings.

TRACK BIO

Location:	**Fort Worth, TX**
Opened:	**1997**
Races hosted:	**Samsung/Radio Shack 500**
Banking/Turns:	**24 degrees/4**
Distance:	**1.5 miles**
Shape:	**Quad-Oval**

RECORDS

Winston Cup Race Record:
T. Labonte 144.276mph
28 March 1999

Winston Cup Qualifying Record:
B. Elliott 194.224mph
31 March 2002

BELOW: Texas is a 1.5-mile superspeedway built in the grandiose style of Charlotte and Atlanta.

Watkins Glen International

A legendary road course, Watkins Glen was host to Formula 1 Racing before the Winston Cup Series returned in 1986.

Few speedways in North America can match the historical significance of Watkins Glen International. The vision of law student Cameron Argetsinger, who spent his summer vacations in the small New York town for which the track is named, Watkins Glen opened in 1948 to host a European-style sports-car race. Though "The Glen" made its reputation in the 1960s and '70s as the site of the Formula 1 United States Grand Prix, the first professional race ever held at the 2.45-mile road course was a Winston Cup event in 1957, when Buck Baker outran Glenn "Fireball" Roberts for the victory.

NASCAR did not hold another race at The Glen until 1964, and after Marvin Panch won the 1965 event in a Ford fielded by the Wood Brothers, 21 years would pass before the Winston Cup Series returned to New York. The late Tim Richmond won the Bud at The Glen in 1986, and NASCAR has been a continuous annual presence ever since. In recent years, the Watkins Glen race has followed the Brickyard 400 in August.

Situated in the Finger Lakes region of New York off County Road 16 in Watkins Glen, the demanding road course has proven popular among fans and drivers alike. Dale Jarrett holds the qualifying record of 122.698 mph, set during time trials for the 2001 Global Crossing at The Glen. In 2002, pole winner Ricky Rudd came within two one-thousandths of a second of matching Jarrett's mark.

TRACK STATISTICS

One of the oldest racks in the United States, this track has also been home to the Formula One US Grand Prix on numerous occasions.

TRACK BIO

Location:	**Watkins Glen, NY**
Opened:	**1948**
Races hosted:	**Sirius Satellite-Radio at the Glen**
Banking/Turns:	**n/a/4**
Distance:	**2.45 miles**
Shape:	**Road Course**

RECORDS

Winston Cup Race Record:
M. Martin 103.030mph
13 Aug. 1999

Winston Cup Qualifying Record:
D. Jarrett 122.698mph
10 Aug. 2001

BELOW: Before stock cars took to the pavement at Watkins Glen, Formula 1 drivers competed on the 2.45-mile road course.

track information

Listed below are the current contact details for all 23 race tracks that will host the 2003 Winston Cup Series.

Atlanta Motor Speedway
P.O. Box 500
Hampton, GA 30228
(770) 946-4211

Bristol Motor Speedway
151 Speedway Blvd.
P.O. Box 3966
Bristol, TN 37625
(423) 764-1161

California Speedway
9300 Cherry Avenue
Fontana, CA 92335
(800) 944-7223

Chicagoland Speedway
500 Speedway Blvd.
Joliet, IL 60433
(815) 727-7223

Darlington Raceway
P.O. Box 500
Darlington, SC 29540
(843) 395-8499

Daytona International Speedway
P.O. Box 2801
Daytona Beach, FL 32120
(386) 253-7223

Dover Downs International Speedway
P.O. Box 843
Dover, DE 19903
(800) 441-7223

Homestead-Miami Speedway
1 Speedway Blvd.
Homestead, FL 33035
(305) 230-7223

Indianapolis Motor Speedway
4790 W. 16th Street
Indianapolis, IN 46222
(317) 481-8500

Kansas Speedway
400 Speedway Blvd.
Kansas City, KS 66111
(913) 328-7223

Las Vegas Motor Speedway
7000 Las Vegas Blvd. North
Las Vegas, NV 89115
(702) 644-4443

Lowe's Motor Speedway
5555 Concord Parkway South
Concord, NC 28027
(800) 455-FANS

Martinsville Speedway
P.O. Box 3311
Martinsville, VA 24115
(276) 956-3151

Michigan International Speedway
12626 U.S. 12
Brooklyn, MI 49230
(800) 354-1010

New Hampshire International Speedway
P.O. Box 7888
Loudon, NH 03307
(603) 783-4931

North Carolina Speedway
P.O. Box 500
Rockingham, NC 28380
(910) 582-2861

Phoenix International Raceway
P.O. Box 13088
Phoenix, AZ 85002
(602) 252-2227

Pocono Raceway
P.O. Box 500
Pocono, PA 18334
(800) 722-3929

Richmond International Raceway
P.O. Box 9257
Richmond, VA 23227
(804) 345-7223

Sears Point (Infineon Raceway)
Highways 37 and 121
Sonoma, CA 95476
(800) 870-7223

Talladega Superspeedway
P.O. Box 777
Talladega, AL 35161
(256) 362-7223

Texas Motor Speedway
P.O. Box 500
Fort Worth, TX 76101
(817) 215-8500

Watkins Glen International
2790 County Route 16
Watkins Glen, NY 14891
(607) 535-2486

Winston Cup 2002 - the Year in Review

The 2002 NASCAR Winston Cup season went from curious to downright strange—and ultimately, to spellbinding. It was the year of a championship no one seemed destined to win, until Tony Stewart started to assume control of the points race at Talladega in October.

It was the year of the most intense and interesting rookie-of-the-year battle in Winston Cup history. Not only did Ryan Newman and Jimmie Johnson vie for supremacy as first-year drivers, but they both also mounted serious threats in the race for the Winston Cup championship.

It was another year of "almost" for Mark Martin, who for the fourth time in his career settled for second place in the championship standings.

It was the year of a title that might have been for Sterling Marlin, the homespun Tennessee native with the "aw, shucks" persona. Marlin lost his momentum in a hard crash at Richmond in September. Three weeks later his season ended with a cracked vertebra in a brutal wreck at Kansas City.

It was the year of emergence for sophomore driver Kurt Busch, who won the first race of his fledgling career at Bristol in April and capped the season with victories in three of the final five events, at Martinsville, Atlanta and Homestead-Miami.

It was the year of triumph for Matt Kenseth, who led the series with five victories. After a 40th-place finish in the June race at Dover, however, Kenseth soon fell from contention for the title.

It was a year in which Dale Earnhardt, Inc., extended its dominance of restrictor-plate racetracks. Dale Earnhardt Jr. won both races at Talladega, and Michael Waltrip scored his lone victory of the season in the Pepsi 400 at Daytona. But the Earnhardt organization was erratic at best at other venues, and Earnhardt, Waltrip and Steve Park played no

ABOVE: Dale Jarrett, Ken Schrader, Elliot Sadler and Dale Earnhardt Jr. in the garage during practice for the NASCAR Winston Cup Pocono 500 on June 7, 2002 at Pocono Raceway in Long Pond, Pennsylvania.

ABOVE: Dale Earnhardt Jr. spins donuts on the infield after winning the Aaron's 499 at Talledega Superspeedway.

dramatic role in the championship race.

It was a year of frustration for Rusty Wallace, who failed to win at least one Winston Cup race for the first time since 1986, when he notched the first of his 54 career victories while driving for owner Raymond Beadle.

It was a year of turmoil for Robert Yates Racing, where conflict and lack of chemistry behind the scenes manifested itself in sub-par performances on the track for drivers Ricky Rudd and Dale Jarrett.

It was a year of disappointment for Travis Carter, whose sponsorship money from bankrupt Kmart ran out after two races, forcing Carter to lose the services of one of his drivers (Joe Nemechek) and to operate on a shoestring until DiscoverCard provided backing for Todd Bodine's car.

It was a year of bewilderment for car owner Ray Evernham, the mechanical guru who had helped Jeff Gordon win three of his four Winston Cup titles.

Expected to lead Dodge to the promised land, Everhman's organization has struggled. No. 1 driver Bill Elliott did win back-to-back races at Pocono and Indianapolis in 2002, but a late-season slump relegated "Awesome Bill" to 13th in points. Evernham and Jeremy Mayfield, driver of the No. 19 Dodge, never seemed to be on the same page in 2002.

It was another year or mediocrity for the once-ascendant Petty Enterprises, which failed to win a race for the third straight year.

It was the year of a bizarre pit crew trade within the Richard Childress organization, a trade that sent Kevin Harvick's crew chief, Kevin Hamlin, to Robby Gordon's team to be replaced by Gordon's crew chief, Gil Martin. The move had a positive effect—but not by much.

It was the year of unexpected explosions, from the haymaker Tony Stewart threw at a photographer in Indianapolis to Busch's tirade against Jimmy Spencer, also at the Brickyard. It was the year NASCAR parked Kevin Harvick for the first Winston Cup event at Martinsville for "conduct unbecoming" during a Craftsman Truck Series race at the same venue.

It was the year of team owner Jack Roush's 60th birthday—one he was lucky to celebrate. Roush was rescued from a lake in Alabama after the private plane he was piloting hit a power line and crashed. Roush's other "pilots"— notably Martin, Busch and Kenseth—enjoyed much more productive seasons.

It was a year of strained relationships. Long-time friend Jimmy Makar announced he would step aside after eight seasons as Bobby Labonte's crew chief. Labonte couldn't keep up with Joe Gibbs Racing teammate Stewart, and lack of team chemistry was the ostensible culprit.

OVERLEAF: View of the Chevy 400 at Richmond, VA on September 7, 2002.

THE HOME DEPOT
Valvoline
DISCOVER 20 DISCOVER
STIHL

2002 Review

LEFT: Bill Elliott crosses the finish line to win the Pennsylavania 500 on July 28, 2002 at Pocono Raceway.

RIGHT: Jeff Gordon celebrates after winning the Mountain Dew Southern 500 on September 1, 2002 at Darlington Speedway.

Jeff Burton, who uncharacteristically brought up the rear in the Roush Racing organization, severed his ties with long-time crew chief Frank Stoddard, who took over as crew chief for Ward Burton (Jeff's brother) after Tommy Baldwin's departure.

Crew chief Michael "Fatback" McSwain and Rudd performed their version of the soap opera "As The Wrench Turns" for the majority of the summer. With Rudd leaving Yates and heading for the Wood Brothers outfit in 2003, McSwain defected to Gibbs Racing to supplant Makar as Bobby Labonte's crew chief. Makar remains as team manager.

The season opened in the wake of Jeff Gordon's highly publicized break-up with wife Brooke, who filed for divorce on the grounds of "marital misconduct." Defending Winston Cup champion Gordon saw his chances for a fifth title disappear late in the season. There are those who say that Gordon's inconsistent performances on the track had less to do with remorse over his split with Brooke and more to do with his newfound liberty.

It was the year of rapid-fire change. "Silly season" didn't wait for its traditional fall arrival. Hirings, firings and resignations altered the landscape of Winston racing as quickly as press releases could be generated to announce them. The end of the 2002 season left myriad drivers, crew chiefs and sponsors with new allegiances for 2003—and several veteran drivers and crew chiefs without jobs for the coming season.

It was the year of NASCAR's youth movement, as Newman, Johnson, Busch and Jamie McMurray brashly announced their arrival. All told, the four prodigies won nine of the Winston Cup Series, 36 points races.

Finally, it was the year whose ending bore no resemblance to its beginning.

Less than three laps into the season-opening Daytona 500 in February, the motor in Tony Stewart's No. 20 Home Depot Pontiac exploded. The first driver to fall out of NASCAR's most prestigious race, Stewart finished 43rd—dead last.

Ward Burton saw the door open for him when Sterling Marlin and Jeff Gordon tangled on lap 194 of 200, with Marlin making a bid for the lead. Gordon spun through the infield grass, and Marlin sustained damage to his right front fender.

After a subsequent 18-car pile-up, NASCAR red-flagged the race for almost 20 minutes to facilitate track cleanup and give the fans at Daytona a green-flag finish. During the stoppage, Marlin climbed from his car and attempted to pull his damaged fender away from the right front tire—an obvious violation of the NASCAR rule that prohibits any work on a car during a red-flag condition.

Penalized for the infraction, Marlin restarted the race from the back of the longest line, and Ward Burton assumed the lead with five laps remaining.

Burton held off Elliott Sadler and Geoffrey Bodine to win his first Daytona 500. As if to fulfill the Biblical prophecy "the first shall be last, and the last shall be first," however, Burton's season began to fall apart while Stewart began a meteoric rise in the points standings.

After the Coca-Cola 600 at Charlotte in May, Burton was 18th and no longer a factor in the championship. Stewart, on the other hand, had

climbed to fifth after four races on the strength of a fourth at Rockingham, a fifth at Las Vegas and a victory at Atlanta.

But it was Marlin who would steal the headlines for much of the season. The 45-year-old veteran from Tennessee took the points lead with a second-place finish at Rockingham in the season's second event, reinforced his position a week later with a win at Rockingham and held it for 25 weeks—until the aftereffects of the crash at Richmond began to take their toll at New Hampshire.

With a 21st-place finish at the New England track, Marlin lost the points lead to Mark Martin on September 15. A week later he dropped from second to fourth with another 21st at Dover. On September 29, Marlin's bid for the title ended abruptly with the crash at Kansas City. A subsequent MRI revealed a cracked C2 vertebra at the base of his skull, and Marlin was sidelined for the rest of the season—a disappointment he endured with extraordinary grace and good humor.

Martin led the championship race for exactly two weeks, until rookie Jimmie Johsnon vaulted into the top spot with a victory at Dover on September 22 followed a week later by a 10th-place finish at Kansas City, where Martin lost the lead with a 25th-place result. The Dover victory was Johnson's third of the season, tying Stewart's record for most wins in a rookie season.

But Johnson's sojourn at the head of the pack was short-lived. The October 6 race at NASCAR's longest superspeedway, Talladega, effectively put an end to his championship aspirations—through no fault of Johnson's.

On the final pace lap for the EA Sports 500, Mark Martin suffered a hydraulic problem in his power steering while turning the wheel back and forth to warm up his tires. The steering column locked, and the No. 6 Viagra Ford veered left into Johnson's No. 48 Lowe's Chevrolet. Johnson pitted as the field took the green flag to start the race, lost a lap on pit road and finished 37th to fall to third in points.

Martin likewise started the event a lap in arrears and struggled to a 30th-place finish and edged Johnson for second in the standings.

Though Dale Earnhardt Jr. won his third straight race at Talladega, the big winner that Sunday was Stewart, who took the championship lead for the first time in his career with an eighth-place finish. Though Stewart struggled with ill-handling cars in two of the final three races, he held the lead the rest of the way and claimed the championship by 38 points over Martin, who had trailed by 112 with two races left on the schedule.

Stewart's title run, however, had no monopoly on drama during the 2002 season. The rookie-of-the-year race between Johnson and Newman was no less intense, as both first-year drivers performed like accomplished veterans. Johnson won three races—at California and at Dover twice. He also won four poles, including the first starting spot for

2002 Review

LEFT: A packed crowd watch the Pepsi 400 on July 6, 2002 at Daytona International Speedway.

RIGHT: Ward Burton celebrates winning the 44th Daytona 500 at Daytona International Speedway in Daytona, Florida.

OVERLEAF: Sterling Marlin driver of the No. 40 Ganassi Racing Dodge Intrepid prepares for another day at the office.

SIMPSON
SIMPSON
BOS
Spark
Snap

Ford
RACING
GOODYEAR
ROUSH
CITGO
NASCAR
Series
tablets
EVENT

2002 Review

ABOVE: Tony Stewart, driver of the No. 20 Home Depot Pontiac, discusses the track conditions with crew chief Greg Zipadelli during practice for the New Hampshire 300, part of the NASCAR Winston Cup Series, at the New Hampshire International Speedway in Loudon, New Hampshire on September 14, 2002.

the Daytona 500.

But Newman won rookie-of-the-year honors on the strength of a more consistent performance. Though Newman won but one race, at New Hampshire in September, he claimed six poles, and his 14 top-five finishes were second only to Stewart's 15. In the Winston Cup championship standings, Johnson and Newman were fifth and sixth, respectively, seven points apart.

For Mark Martin, the 2002 campaign was bittersweet. Though he silenced the critics who had questioned his commitment to winning during a sub-standard 2001 season, he fell one rung short of the series championship for the fourth time in his career.

After the incident with Johnson at Talladega, Martin trailed Stewart by 72 points, with Johnson 82 points behind the leader. A mediocre 16th-place result at Charlotte on October 13 dropped Martin to third behind Stewart and Johnson, 122 points back. Martin kept pace with Stewart a week later at Martinsville, as Johnson regained the 15 points he had lost at Charlotte to trail by 82.

Martin lost ground at Atlanta on October 27, losing 24 points to fall 146 behind Stewart. It was then that the 43-year-old Batesville, Ark., began to apply pressure on Stewart. Martin finished second to first-time winner Johnny Benson at Rockingham and trimmed the Rushville Rocket's lead to 87 points. But Martin's car failed post-race inspection—the left front spring contained four and three-eighths coils instead of the mandated four and a half.

NASCAR docked Martin 25 championship points in a move that was reminiscent of the sanctioning body's action 12 years earlier, when Martin won the early-season race at Richmond but suffered a 46-point penalty for an unauthorized carburetor spacer. Martin lost the championship to Dale Earnhardt by 26 points.

At Phoenix, Martin again cut into Stewart's lead, narrowing the margin from 112 to 89. But when the checkered flag fell at Miami-Homestead, despite Martin's strong fourth-place finish, Stewart nursed his car to an 18th-place showing and secured the championship by 38 points.

"I never really looked at this thing this year and allowed myself to think I would win, and that's a good thing because I feel no letdown now," the stoic Martin said after the final race. "I gave it everything I had from January testing to the last lap today, and I'm not disappointed with the outcome."

LEFT: Mark Martin celebrates winning the Coca-Cola 600 at Lowe's Motor Speedway in Concord, North Carolina on May 26, 2002.

2002 Review

Martin, of course, wasn't the only Roush driver to enjoy an exceptional season. Though traditional stalwart Jeff Burton had a lackluster year, Martin, Busch and Kenseth more than made up for the struggles of their teammate.

Kenseth's season began much like Stewart's, when the 18-car melee at Daytona collected the No. 17 Dewalt Power Tools Ford. But Kenseth won the following week Rockingham to claim the first of what would grow into a series-best five victories. Kenseth was a fixture in the top five in points for the first third of the season, but a disastrous stretch of seven races near mid-season ended his title hopes.

Nevertheless, the 2000 Winston Cup rookie of the year showed his versatility with victories at Rockingham, Texas, Michigan, Richmond and Phoenix as he rallied for the best points finish of his career—eighth.

And what about second-year driver Kurt Busch? With three wins in the final five events of the season, the brash 24-year-old leap-frogged into third place in the Winston Cup standings, right behind Martin, his Roush Racing teammate. With two victories on short tracks (Bristol and Martinsville), one on an intermediate superspeedway (Atlanta) and one on a flat track (Homestead-Miami), Busch gave Winston Cup fans more than a glimpse at the depth of his talent.

And he reinforced the notion that drivers under the age of 35 will be the dominant force in the series for the next few years.

Johnson, Newman, Busch, Stewart, Kenseth and four-time Winston Cup champion Jeff Gordon all fit into that category. Gordon, as defending champion, never felt he performed well enough to win the title, but the failures of others kept him in contention until he finally won his first race of the season at Bristol in August.

That victory only added fuel to the rivalry between Gordon and Rusty Wallace, the two active drivers with far and away the most Winston Cup wins to their credit (Gordon has 61, Wallace 54). Three laps from the finish of the Sharpie 500 at "Thunder Valley," Gordon executed a perfect "bump-and-run" and passed Wallace for the win to break the longest victory drought of his career—31 races.

As it turned out, Bristol was Wallace's best chance to win in a season that brought an end to his streak of 16 straight years with at least one victory.

Gordon carried the momentum from his Sharpie 500 win to Darlington a week later and won his fifth Southern 500, a phenomenal achievement for a driver who had turned 31 less than a month earlier. Gordon left "The Lady in Black" second in points, his high-water mark for the year, but an engine failure at Richmond six days later dropped him to fourth.

Though Gordon won at Kansas City for the second straight season on September 29, the two events surrounding that victory proved the undoing of his title defense. After an early accident at Dover, Gordon finished 37th on September 22, and the week after the Kansas City triumph, he blew an engine at Talladega (as did every other car in the field with a Hendrick motor), came home 40th, and said good-bye to what could have been his fifth championship.

LEFT: Tony Stewart, driver of the No. 20 Joe Gibbs Racing Pontiac Grand Prix, in action on his way toward winning the MBNA 500 at Atlanta Motor Speedway in Hampton, Georgia.

DEWALT
RACING
GOODYEAR
ROUSH Racing
CITGO
DEWALT
.COM
NASCAR
Matt Kenseth

2002 Review

LEFT: Matt Kenseth celebrates after winning the Sirius Satellite Radio 400 on June 16, 2002 at Michigan International Speedway in Brooklyn, Michigan.

ABOVE: Hendrick Motorsports driver Jimmie Johnson (right) is congratulated by co-owner Jeff Gordon after winning the NAPA Auto Parts 500 at the California Speedway in Fontana, California.

PAGES 108/9: Jeff Gordon, driver of the No. 24 Dupont Chevrolet Monte Carlo, during the Sharpie 500 on August 23, 2002 at Bristol Motor Speedway in Bristol, Tennessee.

Winston Cup
Bud
3M

24
DUPONT
PEPSI
GMAC
Fritos
LOWE'S
24

Coors LIGHT
40
TARGET
BROOKS & DUNN
3M

2002 Review

LEFT/RIGHT: Jamie McMurray, driver of the Ganassi Racing Dodge Intrepid, during the UAW-GM Quality 500 on October 10, 2002 at Lowe's Motor Speedway in Concord, North Carolina.

NORTH CAROLINA Speedway
The Rock
POP-SECRET 400
Rockingham, NC Nov. 3, 2002
WINNER
NASCAR
Winston Cup Series
Valvoline
sparco
PONTIAC
PITBULL
Energy Drink

2002 Review

OPPOSITE: Johnny Benson, driver of the Valvoline Pontiac, celebrates winning the Pop Secret Microwave Popcorn 400 on November 3, 2002 at North Carolina Speedway.

ABOVE: Kevin Harvick celebrates after winning the NASCAR Winston Cup Series Tropicana 400 on July 14, 2002 at Chicagoland Speedway in Joliet, Illinois.

LEFT: Kevin Harvick during practice for Sunday's NASCAR Winston Cup Series Aaron's 499 at Talladega Superspeedway in Talladega, Alabama.

PAGES 114/5: Dale Earnhardt Jr. No. 8 and Jeff Gordon No. 24 lead the field during the NASCAR Winston Cup EA Sports 500 at Talladega Superspeedway on October 6, 2002.

Nevertheless, Gordon got plenty of vicarious thrills as co-owner (with Rick Hendrick) of Johnson's No. 48 Chevy. And though Johnson had led his mentor in the points standings for the vast majority of the season, Gordon ran fifth at Homestead-Miami to edge his protégé for fourth place in the final standings by a mere seven points.

Twenty-eight year old Dale Earnhardt Jr., another of NASCAR's prodigies, led 1,068 laps during the 2002 season, more than any other driver. But the performance of Earnhardt and his No. 8 Budweiser team was woefully inconsistent—the son of seven-time Winston Cup champion Dale Earnhardt had to rally late in the season just to finish 11th in points.

Other than a blown right front tire in the Daytona 500, however, there was nothing erratic about Earnhardt's record on NASCAR's two restrictor-plate superspeedways. "Junior" won both races at Talladega to extend his victory streak on the 2.66-mile oval to three events, and he finished sixth in the Pepsi 400 at Daytona—where DEI teammate Michael Waltrip went to Victory Lane for the only time in 2002.

NASCAR's youth movement also made its mark on the 2002 season in an unexpected way. Car owner Chip Ganassi announced he would field a car for Winston Cup rookie Jamie McMurray in 2003, and in doing so,

24
DUPONT
Bud
8
Budweiser
20
NAPA
15
Tide
32
30

CAR Winston Cup Series

2002 Review

Ganassi passed over several drivers with considerably more experience than the confident 26-year-old. It was McMurray who replaced Marlin in the No. 40 Coors Light Dodge after Marlin's crash at Kansas City, and the "young gun" from Joplin, Mo., made an immediate impression.

In his second career start in the Winston Cup Series, McMurray won the UAW-GM Quality 500 at Lowe's Motor Speedway in Charlotte. That victory erased the modern-day record of Kevin Harvick, who had visited Victory Lane in his third career start in 2001.

McMurray, Johnson, Newman and Busch weren't the only first-time winners during one of the most intensely competitive seasons in Winston Cup history. Two weeks after finishing second in the Old Dominion 500 at Martinsville, veteran Johnny Benson won the Pop Secret Microwave Popcorn 400 at Rockingham in his 227th career start.

The 2002 season also marked the end of the road for 35-year veteran Dave Marcis, the owner/driver with the trademark wingtip shoes. Engine failure in the Daytona 500 made Marcis an early casualty, and he bowed out of the Winston Cup Series after 882 career starts. Marcis, however, continued to field his No. 71 in selected races during 2002, with Dick Trickle behind the wheel.

BELOW: Kurt Busch, driver of the No. 97 Rubbermaid Ford Taurus, during the NAPA 500 on October 27, 2002 at Atlanta Motor Speedway in Hampton, Georgia.

RIGHT: Kurt Busch celebrates his first Cup win during the Food City 500 at the Bristol Motor Speedway in Bristol, Tennessee.

OVERLEAF: A view of the stands and the track during the Protection One 400 at the Kansas Speedway in Kansas City, Kansas.

Rubbermaid
PAPER MATE
rmaid
Kurt Busch

76

2002 Review

It was the year of the most intense and interesting rookie-of-the-year battle in Winston Cup history. Not only did Ryan Newman and Jimmie Johnson vie for supremacy as first-year drivers, but they both also mounted serious threats in the race for the Winston Cup championship.

It was another year of "almost" for Mark Martin, who for the fourth time in his career settled for second place in the championship standings.

It was the year of a title that might have been for Sterling Marlin, the homespun Tennessee native with the "aw, shucks" persona. Marlin lost his momentum in a hard crash at Richmond in September. Three weeks later his season ended with a cracked vertebra in a brutal wreck at Kansas City.

It was the year of emergence for sophomore driver Kurt Busch, who won the first race of his fledgling career at Bristol in April and capped the season with victories in three of the final five events, at Martinsville, Atlanta and Homestead-Miami.

It was the year of triumph for Matt Kenseth, who led the series with five victories. After a 40th-place finish in the June race at Dover, however, Kenseth soon fell from contention for the title.

It was a year in which Dale Earnhardt, Inc., extended its dominance of restrictor-plate racetracks. Dale Earnhardt Jr. won both races at Talladega, and Michael Waltrip scored his lone victory of the season in the Pepsi 400 at Daytona. But the Earnhardt organization was erratic at best at other venues, and Earnhardt, Waltrip and Steve Park played no dramatic role in the championship race.

It was a year of frustration for Rusty Wallace, who failed to win at least one Winston Cup race for the first time since 1986, when he notched the first of his 54 career victories while driving for owner Raymond Beadle.

It was a year of turmoil for Robert Yates Racing, where conflict and lack of chemistry behind the scenes manifested itself in sub-par performances on the track for drivers Ricky Rudd and Dale Jarrett.

It was a year of disappointment for Travis Carter, whose sponsorship money from bankrupt Kmart ran out after two races, forcing Carter to

LEFT: Ryan Newman, driver of the No. 12 Alltel/Mobile 1 Ford Taurus, races to win the rain-shortened New Hampshire 300 on September 15, 2002 at the New Hampshire International Speedway.

RIGHT: Tony Stewart lifts the NASCAR Winston Cup Championship trophy at the Ford 400 at the Homestead-Miami Speedway on November 17, 2002.

PAGES 122/3: Tony Stewart on his way to his first Winston Cup Championship..

NASCAR
Winston Cup
Bud
POLE AWARD
MECHANIX WEAR
Holley
HP CARDS
BARNES
3M
Auto Meter
INFOGRAMES
GOODYEAR
BELTS & HOSE
JESEL
EA SPORTS
MAC TOOLS
WM

HOME DEPOT
THE HOME DEPOT
20
MBNA
DAEWOO
CHAMPION
WE CARE
FEL-PRO

2002 Winston Cup Points Standings

Rank	Driver	Points	Starts	Wins	Top 5	Top 10	Winnings
1	Tony Stewart	4800	36	3	15	21	$4,695,150
2	Mark Martin	4762	36	1	12	22	$5,279,400
3	Kurt Busch	4641	36	4	12	20	$3,723,650
4	Jeff Gordon	4607	36	3	13	20	$4,981,170
5	Jimmie Johnson	4600	36	3	6	21	$2,847,700
6	Ryan Newman	4593	36	1	14	22	$4,373,830
7	Rusty Wallace	4574	36	0	7	17	$4,090,050
8	Matt Kenseth	4432	36	5	11	19	$3,888,850
9	Dale Jarrett	4415	36	2	10	18	$3,935,670
10	Ricky Rudd	4323	36	1	8	12	$4,009,380
11	Dale Earnhardt Jr.	4270	36	2	11	16	$4,570,980
12	Jeff Burton	4259	36	0	5	14	$3,863,220
13	Bill Elliott	4158	36	2	6	13	$3,753,490
14	Michael Waltrip	3985	36	1	4	10	$2,829,180
15	Ricky Craven	3888	36	0	3	9	$2,493,720
16	Bobby Labonte	3810	36	1	5	7	$3,851,770
17	Jeff Green	3704	36	0	4	6	$2,135,820
18	Sterling Marlin	3703	29	2	8	14	$3,711,150
19	Dave Blaney	3670	36	0	0	5	$2,677,710
20	Robby Gordon	3632	36	0	1	5	$3,054,240
21	Kevin Harvick	3501	35	1	5	8	$3,748,100
22	Kyle Petty	3501	36	0	0	1	$1,995,820
23	Elliott Sadler	3418	36	0	2	7	$3,390,690
24	Terry Labonte	3417	36	0	1	4	$3,143,990
25	Ward Burton	3362	36	2	3	8	$4,849,880

26	Jeremy Mayfield	3309	36	0	2	4	$2,494,580
27	Jimmy Spencer	3187	34	0	2	6	$2,136,790
28	John Andretti	3161	36	0	0	1	$2,954,230
29	Johnny Benson	3132	31	1	3	7	$2,746,670
30	Ken Schrader	2954	36	0	0	0	$2,460,140
31	Mike Skinner	2886	36	0	0	1	$2,094,230
32	Bobby Hamilton	2832	31	0	0	3	$2,196,960
33	Steve Park	2694	32	0	0	2	$2,681,590
34	Joe Nemechek	2682	33	0	3	3	$2,453,020
35	Casey Atwood	2621	35	0	0	0	$1,988,250
36	Brett Bodine	2276	32	0	0	0	$1,766,820
37	Jerry Nadeau	2250	28	0	0	1	$1,801,760
38	Todd Bodine	1987	24	0	1	4	$1,879,770
39	Kenny Wallace	1868	21	0	0	1	$1,379,800
40	Hut Stricklin	1781	22	0	0	0	$1,313,550
41	Mike Wallace	1551	21	0	0	1	$1,273,240
42	Stacy Compton	1527	21	0	0	0	$1,185,710
43	Geoffrey Bodine	803	10	0	1	2	$1,224,500
44	Steve Grissom	769	10	0	0	1	$529,781
45	Hermie Sadler	688	10	0	0	0	$473,290
46	Jamie McMurray	679	6	1	1	2	$669,097
47	Rick Mast	576	9	0	0	0	$469,843
48	Greg Biffle	570	7	0	0	0	$394,773
49	Buckshot Jones	559	7	0	0	0	$394,223
50	Ted Musgrave	452	5	0	0	0	$283,770

2003 Winston Cup Series

Date	Race	Venue	Pole	Winner
02/09/03	Budweiser Shootout	Daytona Int'l Speedway		
02/13/03	Gatorade 125s	Daytona Int'l Speedway		
02/16/03	Daytona 500	Daytona Int'l Speedway		
02/23/03	Subway 400	North Carolina Speedway		
03/02/03	UAW-DaimlerChrysler 400	Las Vegas Motor Speedway		
03/09/03	Atlanta 500	Atlanta Motor Speedway		
03/16/03	Carolina Dodge Dealers 400	Darlington Raceway		
03/23/03	Food City 500	Bristol Motor Speedway		
03/30/03	Samsung/Radio Shack 500	Texas Motor Speedway		
04/06/03	Aaron's 499	Talladega Superspeedway		
04/13/03	Virginia 500	Martinsville Speedway		
04/27/03	TBA	California Speedway		
05/03/03	Pontiac Excitement 400	Richmond Int'l Raceway		
05/17/03	The Winston	Lowe's Motor Speedway		
05/25/03	Coca-Cola 600	Lowe's Motor Speedway		
06/01/03	MBNA Platinum 400	Dover Int'l Speedway		
06/08/03	Pocono 500	Pocono Raceway		
06/15/03	TBA	Michigan Int'l Speedway		
06/22/03	Dodge/Save Mart 350	Infineon Raceway		
07/05/03	Pepsi 400	Daytona Int'l Speedway		
07/13/03	Tropicana 400	Chicagoland Speedway		
07/20/03	New England 300	New Hampshire Int'l Speedway		
07/27/03	Pennsylvania 500	Pocono Raceway		
08/03/03	Brickyard 400	Indianapolis Motor Speedway		
08/10/03	Sirius Satellite Radio	Watkins Glen International		

08/17/03	**TBA**	**Michigan Int'l Speedway**		
08/23/03	**Sharpie 500**	**Bristol Motor Speedway**		
08/31/03	**Southern 500**	**Darlington Raceway**		
09/06/03	**Chevrolet Monte Carlo 400**	**Richmond Int'l Raceway**		
09/14/03	**New Hampshire 300**	**New Hampshire Int'l Speedway**		
09/21/03	**Dover 400**	**Dover Int'l Speedway**		
09/28/03	**EA SPORTS 500**	**Talladega Superspeedway**		
10/05/03	**TBA**	**Kansas Speedway**		
10/11/03	**UAW-GM Quality 500**	**Lowe's Motor Speedway**		
10/19/03	**Old Dominion 500**	**Martinsville Speedway**		
10/26/03	**Georgia 500**	**Atlanta Motor Speedway**		
11/02/03	**Checker Auto Parts 500**	**Phoenix Int'l Raceway**		
11/09/03	**Pop Secret Popcorn 400**	**North Carolina Speedway**		
11/16/03	**Ford 400**	**Homestead-Miami Speedway**		

Picture Credits

ABOVE: Tony Stewart celebrates winning the 2002 Winston Cup Championship at the Homestead-Miami Speedway.

ALL PICTURES COURTESY OF GETTY IMAGES

PHOTOGRAPHERS WHO CONTRIBUTED WERE:

ROBERT LABERGE, JAMIE SQUIRE, JONATHAN FERREY, DARRELL INGHAM, RUSTY JARRETT, JEFF GROSS, DONALD MIRALLE, CHRIS STANFORD